# NAPOLEON'S BOOK OF FATE

# NAPOLEON'S BOOK of FATE

## The Ancient and Classic Oracle

Michael Colmer

BLANDFORD

**A BLANDFORD BOOK**

First published in the UK by Blandford
A Cassell Imprint
Cassell plc, Villiers House,
41/47 Strand, London WC2N 5JE

Distributed in the United States by Sterling Publishing Co. Inc.
387 Park Avenue South, New York, NY 10016-8810

Distributed in Australia by Capricorn Link (Australia) Pty Ltd
2/13 Carrington Road, Castle Hill, NSW 2154

**British Library in Cataloguing-in-Publication Data**
A catalogue entry for this title is available from
the British Library

ISBN 0-7137-2465-X

Typeset by Litho Link Ltd, Welshpool, Powys, Wales
Printed and bound in Finland by Werner Söderström Oy

# CONTENTS

## THE ORIGINAL NINETEENTH-CENTURY TEXT

# PREFACE

I stumbled on a copy of the 1829 edition of this book while browsing along the shelves of the Atlantis Bookshop, which sits under the watchful eye of the British Museum in London.

The Atlantis, which has an enviable tradition for specialist occult and esoteric publications, had just been acquired by the publisher Psychic Press, whose weekly journal *Psychic News* serves the international Spiritualist community. I had worked as a Spiritualist medium and as a professional astrologer with a personal interest in the history of prophetic divination, and I knew the important role that this book had played in sustaining the oracular tradition: I did not need that small, now-familiar voice at my shoulder urging me to buy it. I am not the first struggling author living in Bloomsbury to be 'guided' to vital works. There have been others before me, and doubtless there are others yet to come. The years passed, and when my publisher issued the scholarly autobiography *Napoleon on Napoleon*, stylishly edited by Somerset de Chair, I felt the same guiding voice say that this was the moment to share this famous Frenchman's personal oracle with a wider audience.

This slim volume that you now hold in your hands began life thousands of years ago as a sacred papyrus buried with a royal mummy in an ancient Egyptian tomb. By chance – or 'fate' – it found its way into Napoleon's hands, and its mysterious answers guided him until he lost it during the battle of Leipzig. Since then, it has passed through many hands and has been lost, found and lost again.

Now you can test it for yourself. Napoleon did, and he would not make a move without it! But remember that oracles are often better judged by what they do not say rather than what they do say. Remember, too, that although Napoleon was born under the zodiac sign of Leo – a sign said to be much given to need appreciation, applause and acclaim – there remains much in this work to offer every reader food for thought.

Michael Colmer

# PROVENANCE

Nostradamus saw him coming. It was some three hundred years earlier, and the old seer certainly did not like what he saw. Those disturbing midnight visions of a close-cropped foreigner associated with the downfall of the French monarchy, with a cavalier attitude to the priesthood and hell-bent on conquering Europe must have given a staunch royalist and devout Catholic such as Michel de Notredame (1503–66) many a sleepless night. But see him in his scrying (or divining) bowl Nostradamus most certainly did, and there are a number of famous quatrains in the *Centuries* to prove it:

*An Emperor will be born near Italy*
*who will cost the Empire very dear*
*The people with whom he mixes will say*
*he will be found less of a prince than a butcher*

*From a simple soldier he will attain the empire*
*From a short robe he will attain the long*
*Valiant in arms, though much worse to the Church*
*To annoy priests as water does the sponge*

*From the marine city held in tribute*
*The shaven-headed man will take his power*
*To put to flight the sordid one who will then oppose him*
*For fourteen years he will maintain his tyranny.*

Napoleon Bonaparte (1769–1821) was born in Corsica and rose to become Emperor, when he opted for the close-cropped, Roman-style hair cut. He recaptured Toulon – 'the marine city' – from the English in 1793; he seized power in a coup d'état against the Directory in November 1799; and he held onto it until his abdication in April 1814 – the fourteenth year.

Just as Magda Goebbels, the wife of Nazi Germany's propaganda minister, later plucked references to 'Hister' from the *Centuries* of

Nostradamus and brought them to the attention of Adolf Hitler, so Napoleon's sycophantic courtiers would have made him aware of the seer's predictions of his success, albeit by a politically selective choice of the appropriate verses.

## The Discovery of the Secret Scroll

Almost two hundred years ago, in 1798, Bonaparte set sail for the Egyptian port of Alexandria. Originally, the campaign plan of the post-Revolutionary French Directory had been to invade Britain. Napoleon persuaded them instead to allow him to direct his efforts to occupy Egypt in order to threaten the lucrative trade between Britain and British India.

In Napoleon's own words: 'The expedition to Egypt had three aims; to establish on the Nile a French colony which would prosper without slaves and serve France in place of the Republic of Santo Domingo and all the sugar islands; to open a market for our manufactures in Africa, Arabia and Syria; and to gain Egypt as a base from which an army of 60,000 men could set out to the Indus to excite these oppressed people to insurrections.'

With Napoleon was a fleet of 350 ships carrying an army of 35,000 troops and supplies. There was also a distinguished band of leading French academics, scientists and historians, all determined to explore the famed treasures of Egypt, and whose findings were eventually published in the monumental eighteen-volume work, *La Description d'Egypte*. According to the story contained in this book, one particular find was kept back for Napoleon's eyes only. Later in this book, this story is told in full as it appeared in the 1822 edition, but modern readers might prefer a precis.

The man who headed the distinguished Commission of Arts accompanying Napoleon, M. Sonnini, discovered a long roll of papyrus attached to the left breast of a mummy 'of extraordinary beauty, and in fine preservation'. Sonnini hastened to Napoleon with his find, and Napoleon gave orders for this mysterious papyrus to be translated. It turned out to be an oracle written by the high priest Balaspis and described as the 'Roll of Man's Fate'.

'None but priests' were permitted to touch this secret papyrus. It was to be preserved in alabaster chests and kept under the temple altar. Copies were permitted to be made for other priests, and it was considered of such importance that it was included in the essential treasures that dead kings were meant to enjoy in their next life. The translator dictated his findings to Napoleon's private secretary, who had strict instructions to interpret the entire papyrus into German to keep it secret from other French eyes.

When he was shown the finished work, Napoleon tested it with his own questions, and in his own handwriting on a blank leaf attached to the translated manuscript were some of his 'test' questions: 'Will my name be immortalized and will posterity applaud it?' And the answer given was: 'Thy name will be handed down, with the memory of thy deeds to the most distant posterity.' This response must have appealed to the superstitious Corsican because, despite admonitions in the explanatory text that the same question should not be asked either on the same day or even twice within the same calendar month, he again tested his new-found oracle with the same question. This time, and in true oracular tradition, the response was just as promising but hedged about with admonition: 'Abuse not the power which the Lord giveth thee, and thy name will be hailed with rapture in future ages.'

Another of Napoleon's questions was: 'Shall I be eminent, and meet preferment in my pursuits?' The answer to this was: 'Thou shall meet with many obstacles, but at length thou shalt attain the highest earthly power and honour.' Hardly an inaccurate response for a man destined to be the Emperor of France and 'Master of Europe'.

There was further encouragement for Napoleon. He asked the oracle: 'What is the aspect of the seasons, and what political changes are likely to take place?' And the reply he received curiously echoed the prophecies of Nostradamus: 'A conqueror, of noble mind and mighty power, shall spring from a low condition: he will break the chains of the oppressed and will give liberty to the nations.'

It is not difficult to see how this man, the son of Carlo Bonaparte who had no fortune and only minor aristocratic connections, would have easily seen himself in the mirror of the oracle's prediction. Despite this, insecurity drove him to repeat the question, but this time the response was more abrupt: 'The wings of the eagle of the north will be clipped and his talons blunted.' This, too, came to pass as predicted but not, coincidentally, until he had lost his personal secret oracle, despite risking his life trying to save it on the battlefield of Leipzig in 1813.

But the answers to his questions appealed greatly to this Leo-born Corsican. So much so that he placed both the original papyrus and the German translation in his own private travelling cabinet, which was constantly at his side. From that time on, we are told in this narrative, before each campaign and on the eve of every battle or treaty, Napoleon consulted his favourite oracle.

After the battle of Leipzig, the oracle was found by a Prussian officer, who, unaware of its importance, sold it for a few napoleons (gold twenty-franc coins) to a French general, who was being held as a prisoner of war in the fortress of Königsburg (Kaliningrad). The general recognized Napoleon's coat of arms on the cover. He knew how much his commander prized the oracle and fully intended to return it to him at the Tuileries as soon as he had recovered from his wounds, but his injuries became gangrenous, and he died before he could return to France.

The oracle was sent to the general's home in France with the rest of his personal effects, and it was eventually restored to the Empress Marie Louise, Napoleon's second wife. But try as she might, it proved impossible to return this highly prized treasure to her husband, who was by this time in exile on St Helena, dictating his memoirs.

Napoleon died on 5 May 1821. It was then that the Empress gave the German interpretator, Herman Kirchenhoffer, permission to translate the oracle into English and to have it published, which he did in London on 1 June 1822. Such was the interest in the oracle that by 1829 there had been no fewer than seventeen editions.

Since then condensed extracts have appeared from time to time in various compilations of works on 'fortune telling', but, to the best of my knowledge, this is the first time in 170 years that the complete translation has been published.

# FACT OR FICTION?

It has been argued that *Napoleon's Book of Fate* was pure invention, and it is possible that this is the case. One precedent lies in the story of similar oracle, the prophecies of the sixteenth-century English seeress, Mother Ursula Shipton.

Greatly feared by the locals of her native Yorkshire, this herbalist, benevolent witch and contemporary 'psychic' is said to have made a series of strange prophecies, including the defeat of the Spanish Armada in 1588; the downfall and death of the highly influential Cardinal Wolsey in the time of Henry VIII; the discovery of vast goldfields in Australia (long before this continent was discovered); the plague that killed thousands and the subsequent Great Fire of London, which cauterized this pestilence.

In the middle of the nineteenth century further prophetic verses, attributed to Mother Shipton, mysteriously appeared. Here are two of them:

> *In nineteen hundred and thirty six*
> *Build houses light with straw and bricks*
> *For then shall mighty wars be planned*
> *And fire and sword shall sweep the land*
> *But those who live the century through*
> *In fear and trembling this shall do*
> *Fleet to the mountains and the dens*
> *To bogs and forest and wild ferns*
> *For storms shall rage and oceans roar*
> *When Gabriel stands on sea and shore*
> *And as he blows his wondrous horn*
> *Old worlds shall die and new be born.*

> *Carriages without horses shall go*
> *And accidents fill the world with woe*
> *Around the earth thoughts shall fly*
> *In the twinkling of an eye*

*Through the hills man shall ride*
*And no horse shall be at his side*
*Under water men shall walk*
*Shall ride, shall sleep, shall talk*
*In the air man shall be seen*
*In white and black and green*
*Iron in the water shall float*
*As easily as a wooden boat.*

But far from being the visions of a sixteenth-century seeress prophesying the outbreak of the Spanish Civil War, the outbreak of the Second World War and the invention of aircraft, wireless telegraphy and submarines, these later verses turned out to be the work of a mischievous Victorian editor, a certain Charles Hindley. Hindley's attempts at deception backfired. His 'invented' prophecies came to pass, and the world did see a war that spawned these new mechnical inventions.

The question this begs is: 'Is *Napoleon's Book of Fate* a similar nineteenth-century invention?' There is certainly no mention of such an oracle in Napoleon's own memoirs, dictated to his generals during his exile on St Helena. Nor, at the time of writing, have I been able to trace any further mention of the high priest Balaspis, from whose hands this oracle is said to have come. In addition, the questions are framed in a decidedly nineteenth-century style.

Against these facts must be set the tone of sincerity, deference and barely concealed academic excitement that pervades the narrative of translator Herman Kirchenhoffer, whom one can easily picture taking painstaking efforts to discharge his duty to the Empress by translating, with Teutonic precision, the oracles into a language that was not his native tongue.

The type of questions, and to some extent their style, set a standard later followed by others, especially the translator of *The Ladies Oracle* by the sixteenth-century astrological physician Heinrich (Henricus) Cornelius Agrippa (1486–1535).

Agrippa was a near contemporary of Nostradamus, and, like the French astrologer, he was forced to ride that precarious rocking-horse that prances between fame and favour before galloping headlong into infamy and persecution. At one time Agrippa was the sought-after confidant and advisor to both the Pope and Emperor Charles V; later, he faced imprisonment for some very unwise predictions.

Agrippa's personal reputation was equally erratic – and erotic. He was regarded as no more than a quack by many, but, like the Russian healer-seer Rasputin, he attracted many susceptible women admirers, some impressed by his gifts, others by his proximity to spiritual power – the 'psychic groupies' of the day.

Claiming himself to be 'an infallible prophet of the male sex', Agrippa penned *The Ladies Oracle* especially for the ladies of the German court to help them through the hopes, joys and tribulations of their love lives. It contained some ninety-five fixed questions, each offering sixteen possible answers, which could be consulted after the appropriate system of divination had been employed.

The original British edition of Agrippa's oracle was published in 1857, some thirty-two years after *Napoleon's Book of Fate*, but the style of the questions bears a strong resemblance to those in the earlier publication. Some of these questions and their responses reflect the preoccupations of men and women since the dawn of time, offering answers to such questions as: 'Shall I live to an old age?' (in *Napoleon's Book of Fate*) and 'Will my old age be passed happily?' (in *The Ladies Oracle*). There is little to choose between 'Will my beloved prove true in my absence?' (*Napoleon's Book of Fate*) and 'The man I love, is he faithful to me?' (*The Ladies Oracle*); or between 'Will my reputation be at all affected by calumny?' (*Napoleon's Book of Fate*) and 'Will my reputation always be good?' (*The Ladies Oracle*).

Every prophet has staunch supporters and hardened sceptics in almost equal measure, and for every person claiming prescience there is a scornful doubter offering rational explanations. Each reader must make up his or her own mind on this matter, but some vestige of proof of any oracle must lie in its testing. Here are thirty-two questions and over a thousand possible answers – test them for yourself and see.

# HOW TO USE THIS ORACLE

## The Historic Method

If you were an Egyptian living at the time the papyrus was originally produced, your access to its prophecies would have been complicated. Gifts would have to be offered and sacrifices made. Then, with all due ceremony, you would have dipped a reed stylus in blood and made a series of random strokes, not just once but five times. These random strokes would have been counted to see which series contained an odd number and which contained an even number. The odd-numbered series produced a one-star symbol; the even series produced two stars. Then, with the forefinger of your left hand you would have traced a question grid, which, in turn, would have offered you a symbol that unlocked the answer.

## The Quick, Modern Method

The fastest way to use this oracle is to select one of the thirty-two questions from the pages that follow and to make a random selection from the symbols on that page. This will give you a number. At the back of the book are the answers, numbered from 1 to 1,024. One of these will be your answer.

It should be said that, although rapid access like this will work most of the time, those traditionalists who prefer to treat their psychic 'tools' with respect will prefer to take their time and will choose the next method.

## The Best Method

This system combines both the historic and the quick, modern access approaches. First, choose your question. Then, with your mind firmly fixed on your query, make a row of quick pen strokes – these can be a series of straight lines or ticks. Do not count them as you do it, but just let your wrist do the work. Tradition dictates that you must make more than twelve strokes.

Repeat this rapidly five times. Now count the number of marks you have made in each row. If the total is an odd number of marks, this will give you one 'star'. If you have made an even number of marks, this will produce two 'stars'. For example:

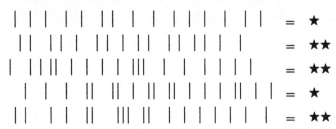

This will give you a 'star' pattern that looks like this:

Now find this pattern on the page that carries your question. This will give you a number between 1 and 1,024. Use this number to find your answer.

If it all seem complex, remember that this is the nature of oracles. Some experts maintain that the more of ritual or random access you introduce, the more accurate the answer. But the test, as always, lies in the response. Sometimes you may not get an answer to the specific question that you thought you were asking. Instead you get an insight, probably very penetrating, into a totally different question altogether. The explanation given for this kind of phenomenon is that while your conscious mind was preoccupied with the chosen question, your subconscious was really wanting answers to a completely different query.

If you try to ask the same question again within a short time – on the same day or during the same week and sometimes even during the same month – it is probable that your subsequent answers could be either abrupt – as Napoleon discovered – or make no sense at all. By tradition, oracles require you to be serious about your question, and they have a tendency to dismiss flippant enquiries. Experts call this 'psychic masturbation', which creates a kind of oracular testiness that results in a psychic 'slapped wrist'.

* * *

Now you are ready to test the oracle for yourself. When it is properly consulted, its responses will amuse, entertain, baffle or astonish you. Remember that this book began life as a sacred papyrus hidden in the bowels of a tomb in ancient Egypt and that Napoleon was so impressed by its accuracy that he risked his life to save it!

THE

# BOOK OF FATE,

FORMERLY IN THE POSSESSION

OF

## NAPOLEON,

LATE

## *EMPEROR OF FRANCE;*

AND

NOW FIRST RENDERED INTO ENGLISH,

FROM A

## 𝔊𝔢𝔯𝔪𝔞𝔫 𝔗𝔯𝔞𝔫𝔰𝔩𝔞𝔱𝔦𝔬𝔫,

OF AN

## ANCIENT EGYPTIAN MANUSCRIPT,

FOUND IN THE YEAR 1801, BY M SONNINI,

IN ONE OF THE

## ROYAL TOMBS,

NEAR MOUNT LIBYCUS, IN UPPER EGYPT.

By H. KIRCHENHOFFER,

FELLOW OF THE UNIVERSITY OF PAVIA, &c. &c. &c

*THE SEVENTEENTH EDITION*

PRINTED FOR C. S. ARNOLD,

21, TAVISTOCK STREET, COVENT GARDEN; AND SOLD BY

MORRISON AND WATT, FENCHURCH STREET; AND C. STOCKING,

3, PATERNOSTER ROW.

1829.

*Publisher's note: the text that follows is reproduced from the 1829 edition of Herman Kirchenhoffer's translation.*

# DEDICATION

TO

HER IMPERIAL HIGHNESS

## MARIE LOUISE,

EX-EMPRESS OF FRANCE, ARCH-DUCHESS OF PARMA, &c. &c.

MADAM,

It is with feelings of the most devout respect and veneration, that, by your Imperial permission, I take the present opportunity of laying the following Work at your Highness's feet.

According to your Imperial Highness's gracious commands, this Translation, although in some passages free (in order to adapt it to the customs of England), is still almost a facsimile of the only and original Manuscript, lately in possession of the ever-to-be-lamented Emperor and King.

In adhering strictly to your Imperial commands, I hope that my endeavours to embellish the Work, according to the original Drawings, will meet with your Imperial Highness's gracious approbation.

With feelings of the most profound Respect,
I remain,
Your Imperial Highness's
Devoted Servant,
HERMAN KIRCHENHOFFER

*London, 1st June, 1822*

# TRANSLATOR'S PREFACE

T HE FOLLOWING Work is translated from a Manuscript, in the German language, which was found among the camp equipage belonging to the late Emperor of France, when he retreated from Leipzic, after the defeat of his army, in the year 1813. It fell to the lot of a Prussian officer, who, ignorant of its great value, sold it for a few Napoleons to a French general officer, then a prisoner of war in the fortress of Konigsburg. This gentleman, aware of its great importance, and knowing from Napoleon's arms, which were emblazoned upon it, that it once belonged to his imperial master, was resolved on his return to France to present it at the Tuileries; but, alas! he did not live to accomplish this purpose; for, although his medical attendants gave him every hope of recovery from his wounds, their efforts to restore him to health proved unavailing, for he died soon after from mortification which took place after amputation of the right arm.

By will, hastily drawn up, the personal effects of this officer were transmitted to his family, who were enjoined to take the earliest opportunity of putting the Manuscript in question into the Emperor's own hands; but Napoleon's manifold occupations, both civil and military, from time to time, prevented this.

During the early part of Napoleon's ostracism in St Helena, means were found of conveying the Manuscript to the Empress, who unfortunately never had an opportunity, although she eagerly sought for it, of sending it to her husband. After his death her Highness gave the Translator her imperial permission for its publication in the English language.

Regarding the purpose which Napoleon had in view in the private perusal of this Work, it is necessary to inform the Reader; but, previous to this, it will be proper to state the manner in which he himself became possessed of it.

It is well known that, in 1801, many French artists and literati accompanied the First Consul in his famous expedition to Egypt, for the purpose of exploring the antiquities of that celebrated region, where once flourished the arts and sciences, in greater perfection than in any other country in the world, the most civilized nations of Europe in the present day, not excepted. At the head of the 'Commission of Arts' was M. Sonnini, whose travels have since excited so much attention. This gentleman, having succeeded in perforating a passage into the interior chamber of one of the royal tombs in Mount Libycus, near Thebes, found therein a sarcophagus, in which was a mummy of extraordinary beauty, and in fine preservation. Having examined this curiosity very minutely, he discovered, attached by a peculiar kind of gum to the left breast, a long roll of papyrus, which, having unrolled, greatly excited his curiosity on account of the hieroglyphics which were beautifully painted on it.

M. Sonnini's description of these tombs, which are of the most astonishing structure, is as follows: 'The whole of the mountain Libycus, which begins at half a league to the west of the Memnonium, and ends immediately opposite to Medinet-abou, is pierced from its base to three-fourths of its elevation with a great number of sepulchral grottos. Those which are nearest the surface of the ground are the most spacious, as well as the most decorated; those which are in the most elevated part of the mountain are much more rudely contrived and executed; while such as hold the middle place, bear an adjusted proportion of space and ornament. Those which belong to the poor are the most interesting, because they always contain some representation of the arts which flourished, and the trades which were practised, at that epoch. The plan of these grottos is in a great measure the same. A door, opening towards the east, displays a gallery of about twenty feet in length, which is sometimes formed in a straight line, and at other times runs off from the entrance in a right angle: it is indifferently supported by columns or pilasters, of which the number varies from four to ten. At the extremity of the gallery are wells which lead to the catacombs, where the mummies are deposited. The depth of these wells varies from forty to sixty feet, and they are connected with long subterraneous passages, rudely shaped in the rock, which terminate in a chamber of about thirty feet square, whose sides are supported by pilasters, and contain large remains of the mummies. There are evident traces of numerous other subterraneous communications, which probably lead to other chambers, that are at present concealed.

'In the upper gallery are sculptured in basso-relievo, or painted in fresco, a crowd of subjects relating to funeral ceremonies. The most interesting pictures which are seen there, offer a detail of circumstances connected with the ancient inhabitants of the country. There, are represented their first occupations, such as the chase and the fishery; thence we may trace the progress of civilization, in the employments of the saddler, the cartwright, the potter, the money-changer, the husbandman, and in the duties and punishments of military life. Each grotto is adorned with a ceiling painted with subjects of fancy, and whose design is exactly the same as that of the paper-hangings which were fashionable in France about thirty years ago.

'The tombs of the kings are about six thousand four hundred paces from the river. They have been formed in a narrow valley, in the centre of the mountain Libycus. The ancient way thither is not known, and the spot is now gained by an artificial passage. These sepulchres occupy a large ravine, which is flanked by the bed of a torrent. The plan of one of these tombs will be sufficient to explain the general disposition of the rest. Every grotto communicates with the valley by a large gate, which opens to a gallery hollowed in the rock: its breadth and height are generally about twelve feet, and its length is twenty paces to the second gate, which opens to another gallery of the same breadth and twenty-four feet in length. To the right and left of this gallery are chambers of five feet in breadth and ten feet long.—There, are found paintings of arms; such as hatchets, poignards, curvated sabres, straight swords, lances, javelins, bows, arrows, quivers, coats of mail, shields, implements of husbandry, vases, and trinkets of every kind. The detail of preparing food is also represented.

'A third gallery succeeds, of the same dimensions as the former, and leads to a chamber above the level of the other apartments, which is eighteen feet square. From this chamber is the entrance to a gallery of thirty-four paces in length; there is also an inclining gallery, whose length is twenty-eight paces. At its extremity is a corridor of sixteen paces, leading to a chamber of eleven paces square, which is connected with another of the same size by a gallery of six paces. A square saloon then succeeds, supported by eight pillars; its length is twenty paces, and its breadth twenty. The Romans made some attempts to carry away this sarcophagus from the grotto where it is deposited; they had even tried to level the ground, in order to facilitate its removal, but they very soon renounced the impracticable enterprise.

'To the saloon of the sarcophagus, another apartment succeeds, of twenty-five paces in breadth, and forty in length. The height of the tomb is seven feet, its length eight, and its breadth six: the total length of the gallery is two hundred and twenty-five paces. The tombs of the kings throughout their whole extent are covered with pictures and hieroglyphics;* but the greater part are painted in

---

* The Egyptian priests, to keep the mysteries of their religion from the knowledge of the common people, used Hieroglyphics, or sacred characters, as the word itself imports, being a Greek compound, signifying 'sacred' and 'to engrave, or carve'.

fresco, and represent the most fantastic subjects that can be conceived. Here it was that the Romans caught that idea of the grotesque, which formed a principal subject of their compositions during the second and third ages of the empire. The researches into Herculaneum have discovered a great number of paintings executed in a similar taste.

'One of the most interesting of these grottos contains a sarcophagus that is still entire and in its place. Its length is sixteen feet, its height twelve, and its breadth six. It still preserves the lid, adorned with the effigy of the king, which is a single block of granite. The astonishment that is felt, on reflecting that this enormous mass was transported to the extremity of a subterraneous passage two hundred paces in length, exceeds all bounds, when it is considered that it was worked upon the place where it remains. What difficulties must have been surmounted, in order to transport a weight of many hundred miliers, across the almost impracticable roads of the mountain!—Here it was that we found the famous mummy and papyrus roll.

'Human sacrifices are continually represented, as well as a diversity of curious Hieroglyphical Figures, one of which represents Isis walking on the Earth, and Flowers springing forth from under her Feet.

'From the time of Strabo, there were reckoned seventeen tombs of kings: and we shall still find the same number, if we comprehend in this enumeration a superb grotto, whose plan is equally large and beautiful with that of the sepulchres of the Theban sovereigns. This grotto is half a league to the north of the Memnonium, and is scooped out at the bottom of a mountain, whose inclosures contain many other tombs: the entrance of several of them is closed, and the greater part of them have been violated. It appears that those, of the ancient Egyptians, who had remained faithful to their worship, endeavoured, from respect to the memory of their princes, to conceal the knowledge of their sepulchres, either from their conquerors, or the professors of other religions.

'The ancient Egyptians, from the king to the lowest of his subjects, were very attentive to the construction of their burying-places, in the firm belief that, after several thousand years, the soul would return to inhabit the body, if, during that time, it should have remained undisturbed. Hence proceeded the custom of embalming, and the position of sepulchres in places inaccessible to the inundation of the river.

'In the neighbourhood of the Memnonium, and amongst the grottos of private individuals, many are found which are still filled with the fragments of mummies. When the Arabs, who consider the grottos as the property of each family, apprehend that they may be visited by strangers, they set fire to the mummies which they contain, in order to turn the curious from the research. There are some of these caverns still untouched; as the persevering traveller has not yet discovered them.

'The sepulchres of the rich are exhausted. None of the mummies which are sold by the people of the country are dressed in the envelope, upon which the figure of Death was painted. A few fragments of these envelopes are all which now appear. It is indeed very extraordinary, that, except in the present instance, no travellers has found the manuscripts on the papyrus, which the mummies of distinguished persons never fail to enclose. These manuscripts are, without contradiction, the most ancient that have been preserved, and appear to contain the prayers made for the dead, and also the mysterious books used by the priests. They are written in hieroglyphics or characters, and are decorated with drawings that resemble the pictures which cover the walls of the sepulchres. Many of the mummies have the nails, both of their hands and feet, gilt. Two rolls of the papyrus are sometimes found with them, which are often placed under the arm-pits, though they are also deposited in the division of the thighs, and near the organs of generation.'

M. Sonnini hastened to the First Consul, whose curiosity, likewise, being much excited by viewing this hieroglyphical treasure, sent for a learned Copt, who, after an attentive perusal, discovered a key whereby he was enabled to decipher the characters. After great labour, he accomplished this task, and dictated its contents to Napoleon's secretary, who, in order to preserve the matter secret, translated and wrote them down in the German language.

The First Consul, having consulted the German translation of the roll regarding some transactions in his own life, was amazed to find that the answers, given, corresponded strictly with what had actually occurred. He accordingly secured the original and translated Manuscripts, in his private cabinet, which ever after accompanied him, until the fatal day of Leipzic above mentioned. They were held by him as a sacred treasure, and are said to have been a stimulus to many of his grandest speculations, he being known to consult them on all occasions. Before each campaign, and on the eve of every battle or treaty, Napoleon consulted his favourite Oracle. His grief for the loss of this companion of his private hours, was excessive; and it is said that, at Leipzic, he even ran the risk of being taken, in his eagerness to preserve the cabinet, containing it, from destruction.

In a list, drawn up in Napoleon's own hand-writing, on a blank leaf prefixed to the translated Manuscript, are to be seen the following Questions, as put to the Oracle, with their Answers, as received, by that illustrious man. They are here selected, from among many others, on account of the very strong analogy, I might say identity, which exists between them and some of the most important actions of his life.

**Question 15** What is the aspect of the Seasons, and what Political Changes are likely to take place?

**Answer** (Hieroglyphic of Cross Keys) 'A conqueror, of noble mind and mighty power, shall spring from low condition; he will break the chains of the oppressed, and will give liberty to the nations.'

**Question 12** Will my Name be immortalized, and will posterity applaud it?

**Answer** (Hieroglyphic of Pyramid) 'Thy name will be handed down, with the memory of thy deeds, to the most distant posterity.'

**Question 8** Shall I be eminent, and meet with Preferment in my pursuits?

**Answer** (Hieroglyphic of Pyramid) 'Thou shalt meet with many obstacles, but at length thou shalt attain the highest earthly power and honour.'

**Question 12** Will my Name be immortalized, and will posterity applaud it?

**Answer** (Hieroglyphic of Castellated Mansion) 'Abuse not the power which the Lord giveth thee, and thy name will be hailed with rapture in future ages.'

**Question 30** Have I any, or many Enemies?

**Answer** (Hieroglyphic of Hand and Dagger) 'Thou hast enemies, who, if not restrained by the laws, would plunge a dagger in thy heart.'

**Question 15** What is the aspect of the Seasons, and what Political Changes are likely to take place?

**Answer** (Hieroglyphic of Castellated Mansion) 'The wings of the eagle of the north will be clipped, and his talons blunted.'

I shall forbear future quotation, as the rest of the answers in the list are either obscure, or relative to matters of inferior or domestic import.

Regarding the personal application of the above answers (except the last, of which I shall speak presently), to the late Emperor, there can be no difference of opinion: this is too obvious to admit of a moment's discussion; indeed, I have been confidently informed, that when he aspired to the imperial throne, he was actually transported with rapture and amazement, when he read the words contained in the Answer to Question 8, viz. 'Thou shalt meet with many obstacles, but at length thou shalt attain the highest earthly power and honour.'

In the second Answer to Question 15, that is, the last which I have quoted from the Emperor's list, the reader will perceive that the Autocrat of Russia is indicated; but whether the words have any direct reference to what passed before the treaty of Tilsit, or to any future boundaries which have been, or may be, opposed to Russian aggrandizement, is not equally certain. At all events, it must be allowed that Napoleon's invasion of the Russian territory clearly proves that his own sentiments were in entire accordance with the latter suggestion.

It had been a happy circumstance for Napoleon, had he uniformly abided, or been ruled by answers to many other questions, which he was in the habit of putting to the Oracle, and which, doubtless, forewarned him of danger, and, most probably, of his downfall: but he was so accustomed, from a long series of success in almost every pursuit which he undertook, to look on the bright side of every circumstance, that, to a mind like his, such forewarnings were not likely to be productive of that salutary restraint which some of his speculations required.

As instances of the lamentable effects of this want of confidence in the oracular counsels contained in the following Work, I may adduce the battle of Leipzic itself, and the fatal consequences of the Russian campaign, viz. the conflagration of Moscow, the destruction of his brave army, and, finally, the abdication of a sceptre which he was long accustomed to wave over the heads of those very monarchs who now compelled him to relinquish it.

To return to the subject of the Manuscripts themselves:— What became of the original Papyrus is not known, but it is supposed that from the frailness of its texture, it was destroyed in the general pillage. If, however, it should be in existence, the present proprietor is hereby earnestly entreated to communicate thereupon with the Secretary of Her Imperial Highness, making whatever demand for its restoration which he may deem requisite;

or he may, if more convenient, deposit it in the Imperial Museum at Vienna, where he shall obtain a receipt for the same in due form. In the care of the administrators of the Museum, he is required to leave a sealed letter, addressed to Her Imperial Highness's Secretary, containing the demand of money, which he feels himself entitled to, in the way of remuneration.

It remains now for the Translator to say something respecting the nature and quality of the Answers which are contained in the BOOK OF FATE. In the first place, then, respecting the nature of the Answers, it will appear that some of these seem to have so direct a reference to the manners and customs of the present age, as almost to deprive them of the same just claims to antiquity which it will be allowed the others undoubtedly possess. But this impression will speedily vanish, when we call to mind, that among the ancient Egyptians the same arts were cultivated, as are now carried on in England and other countries at the present day. Do not the paintings in the tombs, which are still in preservation in Egypt, prove this? It is likewise necessary to take into account, that the work has already passed through two successive translations, consequently, in some passages there must be a considerable deterioration from the original sense; but more particularly, as in phrases of a domestic or professional application, it is sometimes impossible to preserve the real idiom of a translated language.

In my own case, I have to state, that from a long residence in this country, I have been enabled to attain a knowledge of many of the peculiarities both of customs and language among the English people. This knowledge has been of great use in my recent labours, and it will account for those slight deviations which I have some-times found necessary, in adapting an ancient Egyptian work to modern eyes and ears. These deviations, however, are few, and, I may add, slight; but they will be more certainly appreciated when the Reader has had an opportunity of perusing the present translation, and then comparing it with the German and French ones, which I intend to have published immediately on my return to the Continent.

In the second place, regarding the quality of the Answers, I have to observe, that they are of five kinds, viz. positive, mandatory, presumptive, admonitory, and conditional. As examples, I shall select five, (that is, one of each quality,) from among seventeen, which have been returned to various persons who consulted the Oracle since it has been in my possession.

First, then, of the positive. It was asked (Question 17) by a gentleman, 'Will my beloved prove true in my absence?' The Answer returned was (Hieroglyphic of the Plough) 'The affections of the being whom thou lovest, will be placed on none other but thyself.'

Example of the mandatory. It was asked (Question 6) 'Shall I make, or mar, my fortune by gambling?' The Answer was (Hieroglyphic of Cross Bones) 'Be warned! from henceforth, never play for money, nor money's worth.'

As an example of the presumptive, it was asked (Question 28) 'Shall I ever find a treasure?' The answer was such as to leave no doubt on the consulter's mind that he should find a treasure; but at the same time it contained such good counsel, as to the application of it, as was absolutely required of a man of his circumstances and disposition. It was (Hieroglyphic of Fasces) 'When thou findest a treasure, teach thy tongue to be silent; and see that thou makest good use of thy riches.'

To exemplify the admonitory, I may give an instance of a lady who consulted the Oracle in the following words (Question 24) 'Inform me of all particulars relating to my future husband.' The Answer was (Hieroglyphic of the Bow and Arrow) 'Consider well whether thou oughtest, at present, to change thy condition in life.'

Lastly, as an example of the conditional Answers, I select the following. It was asked (Question 19) by the mother of a large family, 'After my death will my children be virtuous and happy?' The Answer was (Hieroglyphic of the Ladder) 'In the training of thy offspring, let thy discipline be strict, but not severe; lose no opportunity of improving their understandings, and, in the plenitude of their happiness, they will bless thee.'

Another quality which pertains to a few of these Answers, is the close affinity which seems to exist between them and some of the most favourite moral axioms in use among the civilized nations of antiquity: but is this to be wondered at, when we consider that Egypt had long been the residence of the Hebrews, and that it had been overrun both by the Greeks and Romans, who afterwards formed settlements there? It cannot be doubted, therefore, that the Hebrews not only retained the arts which they saw cultivated, and learned, in Egypt, but also that their priests became possessors of copies of books which were in use in the temples. That the Greeks and Romans did so, is beyond speculation; for it is well known (being asserted by Herodutus and other historians) that all the Oracles, afterwards established in the states of Greece, and elsewhere, owed their origin to books found in the Egyptian temples, which were pillaged and plundered upwards of 3000 years ago. That these books were mere transcripts of the original copy of the work now given to the world, there can likewise be no doubt; consequently, the inference is a fair one, that, the moral axioms, above spoken of, were borrowed from these books, and that, being greatly admired by the literati of those days, such passages were afterwards transplanted into their own works, as original.

This explanation of the apparent identity will be perfectly satisfactory to every candid reader; but, in order to throw as much light on the subject as possible, I have prefixed to the present work an authentic and interesting account of the ORACLES which bore so famous a part in the histories of ancient Egypt and Greece.

The Translator, in taking his leave of the British Public, has now merely to state that the BOOK OF FATE, in its English dress, is adapted to all conditions of life; and persons of every rank and capacity will now have an opportunity of consulting it, and of regulating their future conduct according to its ORACULAR COUNSELS.

H. KIRCHENHOFFER
London, June 1, 1822

# INTRODUCTORY ACCOUNT OF ANCIENT ORACLES

No INSTITUTION is more famous than the ancient Oracles of Egypt, Greece and Rome. They were said to be the will of the gods themselves, and they were consulted, not only upon every important matter, but even in the affairs of private life. To make peace or war, to introduce a change of government, to plant a colony, to enact laws, to raise an edifice, or to marry, were all sufficient reasons to consult the will of the gods. Mankind, in consulting them, showed that they wished to pay implicit obedience to the command of the divinity, and, when they had been favoured with an answer, they acted with more spirit, and with more vigour, conscious that the undertaking had met with the sanction and approbation of heaven. In this, therefore, it will not appear wonderful that so many places were sacred to oracular purposes.

The small province of Boeotia could once boast of her 25 oracles, and Peloponnesus of the same number. Not only the chief of the gods gave oracles, but, in process of time, heroes were admitted to enjoy the same privileges; and the oracles of a Trophonius and an Antinous, were soon able to rival the fame of Apollo and of Jupiter. The most celebrated oracles of antiquity were those of Dodona, Delphi, Jupiter Ammon, &c. The temple of Delphi seemed to claim a superiority over the other temples; its fame was once more extended, and its riches were so great, that not only private persons, but even kings and numerous armies, made it an object of plunder and of rapine.

The manner of delivering oracles was different. A priestess at Delphi was permitted to pronounce the oracles of the god, and her delivery of the answers was always attended with acts of apparent madness and desperate fury. Not only women, but even doves, were the ministers of the temple of Dodona; and the suppliant votary was often startled to hear his questions readily answered by the decayed trunk, or the spreading branches of a neighbouring oak. Ammon conveyed his answers in a plain and open manner; but Amphiarius required many ablutions and preparatory ceremonies, and he generally communicated his oracles to his suppliants in dreams and visions. Sometimes the first words that were heard, after issuing from the temple, were deemed the answers of the oracles, and sometimes the nodding or shaking of the head of the statue, the motions of fishes in a neighbouring lake, or their reluctance in accepting the food which was offered to them, were as strong and valid as the most express and most minute explanations.

It is a question among the learned, whether the oracles were given by the inspiration of evil spirits, or whether they proceeded from the imposture of the priests. Imposture, however, and forgery, cannot long flourish, and falsehood becomes its own destroyer; and on the contrary, it is well known how much confidence the people, even of an enlightened age, place upon dreams, prophecies, and unaccountable incidents. Some have strongly believed that all the oracles of the earth ceased at the birth of Christ, but the supposition is false. It was, indeed, the beginning of their decline; but they remained in repute, and were consulted, though perhaps not so frequently, till the fourth century, when Christianity began to triumph over paganism. The oracles often suffered themselves to be bribed. Alexander did it, but it is well known that Lysander failed in the attempt. Herodotus, who first mentioned the corruption which often prevailed in the oracular temples of Greece and Egypt, has been severely treated for his remarks, by the historian Plutarch. Demosthenes is also a witness of the corruption, and he observed, that the oracles of Greece were servilely subservient to the will and pleasure of Philip king of Macedon, as he beautifully expressed it by the word *Philipidzein.*

When in a state of inspiration, the eyes of the Priestess suddenly sparkled, her hair stood on end, and a shivering ran all over her body. In this convulsive state she spoke the oracles of the god, often with loud howlings and cries, and her articulations were taken down by the priest, and set in order. Sometimes the spirit of inspiration was more gentle, and not always violent; yet Plutarch mentions one of the priestesses who was thrown into such an excessive fury, that not only those that consulted the oracle, but also the priests that conducted her to the sacred tripod, and attended her during the inspiration, were terrified and forsook the temple; and so violent was the fit, that she continued for some days in the most agonizing situation, and at last died. At Delphos, the Pythia, before she placed herself on the tripod, used to wash her whole body, and particularly her hair, in the waters of the fountain Castalis, at the foot of mount Parnassus. She also shook a laurel tree that grew near the place, and sometimes ate the leaves, with which she crowned herself.

The Priestess always appeared dressed in the garments of virgins to intimate their purity and modesty, and they were solemnly bound to observe the strictest laws of temperance and chastity, that neither fantastical dresses nor lascivious behaviour might bring the office, the religion, or the sanctity of the place into contempt. There was originally but one Pythia, besides subordinate priests, but afterwards two were chosen, and sometimes more. The most celebrated of all these is Phemonoe, who is supposed by some to have been the first who gave oracles at Delphi. The oracles were always delivered in hexameter verses, a custom which was some time after discontinued. The Pythia was consulted only one month in the year, about the spring. It was always required, that those who consulted the oracle should make large presents to Apollo, and from thence arose the opulence, splendour, and the magnificence of the celebrated temple of Delphi. Sacrifices were also offered to the divinity, and if the omens proved unfavourable, the priestess refused to give an answer. There were generally five priests who assisted at the offering of the sacrifices, and there was also another who attended the Pythia, and assisted her in receiving the oracle.

We shall now proceed to describe some of the most celebrated of the ancient Oracles:

## ORACLE OF DELPHOS

Delphos, now called Castri, the capital of Phocis, in Greece, was anciently much celebrated for its Temple and Oracle of Apollo. It was also called Pytho, by the poets; from the serpent Python, which Apollo killed in this place. Pausanias, however, says that this name pytho was given to the city of Delphos, by Pythis, son of Delphus, and grandson of Lycorus. The Greek historians gave to this city the name of Delphos, which some suppose to have been so called from Adelphoi, brethren, because Apollo and his brother Bacchus were both worshipped there; and others, with greater probability, derive the name from Delphos, single, or solitary, referring to the retired situation of the city among the mountains.

Justin questions, which was the most worthy of admiration, the fortification of the place, or the majesty of the god, who here delivered his oracles. The Temple of Apollo occupied a large space, and many streets opened to it. The first discovery which laid the foundation of the extraordinary veneration in which the Oracle of Delphos was held, and of the riches accumulated in the temple, is said to have been occasioned by some goats which were feeding on mount Parnassus, near a deep and large cavern, with a narrow entrance. These goats having been observed by the goat-herd,

Coretas, to frisk and leap after a strange manner, and to utter unusual sounds immediately upon their approach to the mouth of the cavern, he had the curiosity to view it, and found himself seized with the like fit of madness, skipping, dancing, and foretelling things to come.

At the news of this discovery, multitudes flocked thither, many of whom were possessed with such frantic enthusiasm that they threw themselves headlong into the opening of the cavern; insomuch, that it was necessary to issue an edict, forbidding all persons to approach it. This surprising place was treated with singular veneration, and was soon covered with a kind of chapel, which was originally made of laurel boughs, and resembled a large hut. This, according to the Phocian tradition, was surrounded by one of wax, raised up by bees. After this a third was built of solid copper, said to have been the workmanship of Vulcan.

This last was destroyed, by an earthquake, or, according to some authors, by fire, which melted the copper; and then a sumptuous Temple, altogether of stone, was erected by two excellent architects, Trophimus and Agamedes. This edifice was destroyed by fire in the 58th Olympiad, or 548 years B.C. The Amphictyons proposed to be at the charge of building another; but the Alcmeonides, a rich family of Athens, came to Delphos, obtained the honour of executing the building, and made it more magnificent than they had at first proposed. The riches of this Temple, amassed by the donations of those who frequented it and consulted the Oracle, exposed it to various depredations. At length the Gauls, under the conduct of Brennus came hither for the same purpose, about 278 years B.C.; but they were repulsed with great slaughter. Last of all, Nero robbed it of 500 of its most precious brazen and golden statues.

It has not been ascertained at what time this Oracle was founded. It is certain, however, that Apollo was not the first who was consulted here. Aeschylus, in his tragedy of the Eumenides, says, Terra was the first who issued oracles at Delphi: after her Themis, then Phoebe, another daughter of Terra, and as it is said, mother of Latona, and grandmother to Apollo. Pausanias says, that before Themis, Terra and Neptune had delivered oracles in this place, and some say that Saturn had also been consulted here. At length the Oracle of Apollo became established and permanent; and such was its reputation, and such were the multitudes from all parts that came to consult it, that the riches which were thus brought into the temple and city, became so considerable as to be compared with those of the Persian kings.

About the time when this Oracle was first discovered, the

whole mystery requisite for obtaining the prophetic gift, is said to have been merely to approach the cavern and inhale the vapour that issued from it; and then the god inspired all persons indiscriminately; but at length several enthusiasts, in the excess of their fury, having thrown themselves headlong into the cavern, it was thought expedient to contrive a prevention of this accident, which frequently occurred. Accordingly, the Priests placed over the hole, whence the vapour issued, a machine which they called 'a tripod', because it had three feet, and commissioned a woman to seat herself in it, where she might inhale the vapour without danger, because the three feet of the machine stood firmly upon the rock. This Priestess was named Pythia, from the serpent Python, slain by Apollo, or from the Greek *puthesthai*, signifying to inquire, because people came to Delphi to consult this deity. The females, first employed, were virgins selected with great precaution; but the only qualification necessary was to be able to speak and repeat what the god dictated.

This was done by placing her ear close to one of the horns of the altar, and listening to the voice of one of Apollo's priests, to whom the question had been communicated. This Priest, who stood near the altar, in the interior of the Temple, having been assisted by his brethren in the necessary devotions and sacrifices opened the BOOK OF FATE, which was deposited in the Temple, and after many prayers, worked the required problems. The ANSWER, which from the nature of the case in hand, was often conditional, being communicated to the Priestess on the tripod was, after various ceremonies, delivered to the enquiring multitude, or to the individual who came privately to consult the Oracle.

The custom of choosing young virgins continued for a long time, till one of them, who was extremely beautiful, was dishonoured by a young Thessalian. An express law was then enacted, that none should be chosen but women above fifty years old. At first there was only one Priestess, but afterwards, there were two or three. The oracles were not delivered every day; but gifts and sacrifices were in some cases presented for a long time, and even for a whole year; and it was only once a year in the month bosion, which answered to the beginning of spring, that Apollo inspired the Priestess. Except on this day she was forbidden, under pain of death, to go into the sanctuary to consult Apollo.

Alexander, before his expedition into Asia, came to Delphi on one of those days when the sanctuary was shut, and intreated the Priestess to mount the tripod, which she steadily refused, alleging the law which forbade her. The prince, naturally impetuous, became impatient, and drew the Priestess by force from her cell, and whilst he was conducting her to the sanctuary, she took occasion to exlaim, 'MY SON, THOU ART INVINCIBLE!!' As soon as these words were pronounced, Alexander cried out that he was satisfied, and would have no other oracle.

It is here to be observed, however, that great but unnecessary preparations were often made for giving mysteriousness to the oracle, and for commanding the respect that was paid to it. Among other circumstances relating to the sacrifices that were offered, the Priestess herself fasted three days, and before she ascended the tripod, she bathed herself in the fountain of Castala. She drank water from that fountain, and chewed laurel-leaves gathered near it. She was then led into the sanctuary by the priests, who placed her upon the tripod.

As soon as she began to be agitated by the divine exhalation, said to arise from the cavern, but which was merely the vapour of incense burnt there, in order to give more mystery to the affair, her hair stood on end, her aspect became wild and ghastly, her mouth began to foam, and her whole body was suddenly seized with violent tremblings. In this condition she attempted to escape from the Priests, who detained her by force, while her shrieks and howlings made the whole temple resound, and filled the by-standers with a sacred horror.

At length, unable to resist the impulse of the god, she surrendered herself up to him, and at certain intervals uttered from the bottom of her stomach, or belly, by the faculty or power of ventriloquism, some unconnected words, which the Priests ranged in order, and, put in form of verse, giving them a connection which they had not when they were delivered by the Priestess. The oracle being pronounced, the Priestess was taken off the tripod, and conducted back to her cell, where she continued several days to recover herself. Lucan tells us, that speedy death was frequently the consequence of her enthusiasm. The oracles pronounced by the Priestess being generally delivered to the poets, who attended on the occasion, and being put by them into wretched verse, gave occasion to the raillery, that Apollo the Prince of the muses, was the worst of poets.

The Priests and Priestesses, to whose conduct the responses of the Oracle were committed, were however, frequently guilty of fraud and imposture. And many instances might be mentioned, in which the Delphic Priestess was not superior to corruption. Hence she persuaded the Lacedaemonians to assist the people of Athens in the expulsion of the 30 tyrants. Hence, also, she caused Demaratus to be divested of the royal dignity to make way for Cleomenes; and supported the imposter Lysander, when he endeavoured to change the succession to the throne of Sparta. It is not improbable, that Themistocles, who well knew the importance of acting against the Persians by sea, inspired the god with the answer he gave, 'to defend themselves with walls of wood.'

These answers were likewise, on many occasions equivocal. Thus, when Croesus was about to invade the Medes, he consulted this Oracle upon the success of the war, and received for answer, that by passing the river Halys, he should win a great empire. But he was left to conjecture, or to determine by the event, whether this empire was his own or that of his enemies. Such was also the same Oracle's answer to Pyrrhus, 'Aio te, Aeacid, Romanos vincere posse.' which meant, 'I say unto thee, O Greek, thou canst overcome the Romans,' or, 'I say unto thee, the Romans may overcome the Greeks.'

## ORACLE OF DELOS

The Oracle of Apollo, in Delos, was one of the most famous Oracles in the world, not only for its antiquity, but for the richness of the sacred presents dedicated to the god, and the numbers of persons that resorted hither from all parts for advice; in which respect it surpassed not only all the Oracles of other gods, but even those of Apollo, himself,—that of Delphos alone excepted. Some writers say, that the island had the name of Delos, from the clear and simple terms in which the answers were here given by the Oracle, contrary to the ambiguity observed in other places; but it was consulted only while Apollo made Delos his summer residence, for his winter abode was at Patara, a city of Lycia. The presents offered by the votaries to Apollo, were laid on the altar, which, as some say, was erected by Apollo himself, when he was only four years old, and formed of the horns of goats, killed by Diana, on mount Cynthus. It was preserved pure from blood and every kind of pollution, as offensive to Apollo. The whole island was an asylum, which extended to all living creatures, dogs excepted, which were not suffered to be brought on shore.

The native deities, Apollo and Diana, had three very magnificent temples erected for them in this island. That of Apollo, was, according to Strabo, (lib. x.) begun by Erysiapthus, the son of Cecrops, who is said to have possessed this island 1558 years B.C.; but it was afterwards much enlarged and embellished at the general charge of all the Grecian states. But Plutarch says, that it was one of the most stately buildings in the universe, and describes its altar, as deserving a place among the seven wonders of the world. The inscription in this temple, as Aristotle informs us,

(*Ethic.* 1.i.c.9.) was as follows: 'Of all things the most beautiful is justice; the most useful is health; and the most agreeable is the possession of the beloved object.'

Round the temple were magnificent porticoes, built at the charge of various princes, as appears from the still legible inscriptions. To this temple the neighbouring islands sent yearly a company of virgins to celebrate with dancing the festival of Apollo, and his sister Diana, and to make offerings in the name of their respective cities.

Delos was held in such reverance by most nations, that even the Persians, after having laid waste the other islands, and everywhere destroyed the temples of the gods, spared Delos; and Datis, the Persian admiral, forbore to anchor in the harbour.

## ORACLE OF AMMON

The Temple of Jupiter Ammon was in the deserts of Libya, nine days journey from Alexandria. It had a famous Oracle, which, according to ancient tradition, was established about 18 centuries before the time of Augustus, by two doves which flew away from Thebais in Egypt, and came, one to Dodona, and the other to Libya, where the people were soon informed of their divine mission. The Oracle of Ammon was consulted by Hercules, Perseus, and others; but when it pronounced Alexander to be the son of Jupiter, such flattery destroyed its long established reputation, and in the age of Plutarch it was scarcely known. The situation of the temple was pleasant; and there was near it a fountain whose waters were cold at noon and midnight, and warm in the morning and evening. There were about 100 priests in the temple, but the elders only delivered oracles. There was also an Oracle of Jupiter Ammon in Aethiopia.

## ORACLE OF DODONA

Dodona was a town of Thresprotia in Epirus. There was in its neighbourhood, upon a small hill called Tmarus, a celebrated Oracle of Jupiter. The town and temple of the god were first built by Deucalion, after the universal deluge. It was supposed to be the most ancient Oracle of all Greece, and according to the traditions of the Egyptians mentioned by Herodotus, it was founded by a dove. Two black doves as he relates, took their flight from the city of Thebes, in Egypt, one of which flew to the temple of Jupiter Ammon, and the other to Dodona, where with a human voice they acquainted the inhabitants of the country that Jupiter had consecrated the ground, which in future would give oracles. The extensive grove which surrounded Jupiter's temple was endowed with the gift of prophecy, and oracles were frequently delivered by the sacred oaks, and the doves which inhabited the place. This fabulous tradition of the oracular power of the doves, is explained by Herodotus, who observes that some Phoenicians carried away two priestesses from Egypt, one of which went to fix her residence at Dodona, where the Oracle was established. It may further be observed, that the fable might have been founded upon the double meaning of the word peleiai, which signifies doves in most parts of Greece, while in the dialect of the Epirots, it implies old women. In ancient times the oracles were delivered by the murmuring of a neighbouring fountain, but the custom was afterwards changed. Large kettles were suspended in the air near a brazen statue, which held a lash in its hand. When the wind blew strong, the statue was agitated and struck against one of the kettles, which communicated the motion to all the rest, and raised that clattering and discordant din which continued for a while, and from which the priests drew their predictions. Some suppose that the noise was occasioned by the shaking of the leaves and boughs of an old oak, which the people frequently consulted, and from which they pretended to receive the oracles. It may be observed with more probability that the oracles were delivered by the priests, who, by concealing themselves behind the oaks, gave occasion to the multitude to believe that the trees were endowed with the power of prophecy. As the ship Argo was built with some of the oaks of the forest of Dodona, there were some beams in the vessel which gave oracles to the Argonauts, and warned them against the approach of calamity. Within the forest of Dodona there was a stream with a fountain of cool water, which had the power of lighting a torch as soon as it touched it. This fountain was totally dry at noon day, and was restored to its full course at midnight, from which time till the following noon it began to decrease, and at the usual hour was again deprived of its waters. The oracles of Dodona were originally delivered by men, but afterwards by women.

## THE ROMAN AUGURS

The Augurs were certain Priests at Rome who foretold future events, whence their name, ab avium garritu. They were first created by Romulus to the number of three. Servius Tullius added a fourth, and the tribunes of the people A.U.C. 454, increased the number to nine; and Sylla added six more, during his dictatorship. They had a particular college, and the chief amongst them was called Magister Collegii. Their office was honourable; and if any one of them was convicted of any crime, he could not be deprived of his privilege; an indulgence granted to no other sacerdotal body at Rome. The augur generally sat on a high tower, to make his observations. His face was turned towards the east, and he had the north to his left, and the south at his right. With a crooked staff he divided the face of the heavens into four different parts, and afterwards sacrificed to the gods, covering his head with his vestment. There were generally five things from which the augurs drew omens: the first consisted in observing the phenomena of the heavens, such as thunder, lightning, comets, &c. The second kind of omen was drawn from the chirping or flying of birds. The third was from the sacred chickens, whose eagerness or indifference in eating the bread which was thrown to them, was looked upon as lucky or unlucky. The fourth was from quadrupeds, from their crossing or appearing in some unaccustomed place. The fifth was from different casualties, which were called Dira, such as spilling salt upon a table, or wine upon one's clothes, hearing strange noises, stumbling or sneezing, meeting a wolf, hare, fox, or pregnant bitch. Thus did the Romans draw their prophecies; the sight of birds on the left hand was always deemed a lucky object, and the words sinister & loevus, though generally supposed to be terms of ill luck, were always used by the augurs in an auspicious sense.

## THE SIBYLLINE BOOKS

A strange old woman came once to Tarquinius Superbus, king of Rome, with nine books, copies of the following work, which she said were the ORACLES OF THE SIBYLS, and proffered to sell them. But the king making some scruple about the price, she went away and burnt three of them; and returning with the six, asked the same sum as before. Tarquin only laughed at the humour; upon which the old woman left him once more; and after she had burnt three others, came again with those that were left, but still kept to her old terms. The king began now to wonder at her obstinancy, and thinking there might be something more than ordinary in the business, sent for the Augurs to consult what was to be done. They, when their divinations were performed, soon acquainted him what a piece of impiety he had been guilty of, by refusing a treasure sent to him from heaven, and commanded him to give whatever she demanded for the books that remained. The woman received her money, and delivered the writings, and only charging them by all means to keep them sacred, immediately vanished. Two of the nobility were presently after chosen to be the keepers of these oracles, which were laid up with all imaginable care in the capitol, in a chest under ground. They could not be consulted without a special order of the senate, which was never granted, unless upon the receiving some notable defeat, upon the rising of any considerable mutiny or sedition in the state, or upon some other extraordinary occasion.

The number of priests, in this, as in most other orders, was several times altered. The Duumviri continued till about the year of the city 388, when the tribunes of the people preferred a law, that there should be ten men elected for this service, part out of the nobility, and part out of the commons. We meet with the Decemviri all along from hence, till about the time of Sylla the dictator, when the Quindecemviri occur. It were needless to give any farther account of the Sibyls, than that they are generally agreed to have been ten in number; for which we have the authority of Varro; though some make them nine, some four, some three, and some only one. They all lived in different ages and countries, were all prophetesses; and, according to common opinion, foretold the coming of our Saviour. As to the writing, Dempster tell us it was on linen.

Solinus acquaints us, that the books which Tarquin bought, were burnt in the conflagration of the capitol, the year before Sylla's dictatorship. Yet there were others of their inspired writings, or at least copies or extracts of them, gathered up in Greece and other parts, upon a special search made by order of the senate; which were kept with the same care as the former, till about the time of Theodosius the Great, when, the greatest part of the senate having embraced the Christian faith, they began to grow out of fashion; till at last Stilicho burnt them all, under Honorius, for which he is severely censured by the poet Rutilius.

# THE WRITING OF BALASPIS
## By Command of
## Hermes Trismegistus
## Unto the Priests of the Great Temple

PRIESTS OF THEBAIS! Servants in the great temple of HECAT-OMPYLOS! Ye who in the sacred city DIOSPOLIS, have dedicated your lives to the services of the King of the Gods and of men! HERMES,* the interpreter of the will of OSIRIS, greets you!

It is the will of the Gods, in grand assembly convened, that ye preserve your lives free from stain and pollution.

It is their will that ye continue to instruct the nations, as far as they may be permitted to know.

It is the pleasure of OSIRIS, sitting on his throne of clouds, and surrounded by the inferior deities, that ye make known to his subjects, his children upon earth, whatever may concern their DESTINY, and what matters ye shall find written in the book of books:—THE WRITTEN ROLL OF MAN'S FATE, now committed to your safe keeping:—that ye do this strictly and truly, without fear of danger, or hope of reward, according to all questions that may be asked, by individual persons, by tribes, by rulers of state, and by conquerors of nations.

OSIRIS commandeth the servants in his favoured sanctuary to shew favour unto none, in the answers which it will be their duty to give from this book. Let sacrifices and gifts and invocations be made; let the question be asked in all humility and strong faith, and when the DIVINER hath consulted the winding and intricacies of the problem, according to the instructions hereunto appended, let

---

* To Hermes Trismegistus, a sage as highly revered among them, as Zoroaster was among the Persians, the Egyptians ascribed the inventions of chief use to human life; and like every people who are unable to settle the antiquity of their origin, they represented his works to have outstood the shock even of the universal deluge. They otherwise called him Thoth; and their priests constantly maintained that from the hieroglyphical characters upon the pillars he erected, and the sacred books, all the philosophy and learning of the world has been derived, and all the oracular intelligence has been drawn.

the result be written and handed to the chief PROPHET OR PROPHETESS, (seated on a stool having three legs); who shall read and interpret the writing of Hermes unto the enquirer, in the face of all the assembled people.

And the PROPHET OR PROPHETESS shall read no writing but what hath been truly given to her by the priest who doth officiate in the sacrifice; and the priest shall not add to, nor diminish from, what he findeth to be the true answer to the question asked, as in this ROLL OF MAN'S FATE contained: neither shall he substitute one answer for another, but in all things he shall do according to the instructions herein given.

The highest among the Gods, in like way, ordaineth, that no bribe, nor private gift, shall be offered or taken, either by the individual who enquireth, or by the priest who maketh answer to the consultation: let the gift, which is to be offered, be of free will, and let it be put upon the altar after the sacrifice hath been consumed, in the face of all people. If herein the priests offend, they shall, on the instant, be struck down and pinioned to the earth by the piercing and fiery arrows which the great OSIRIS in his anger, speaking from the clouds, hurleth at offending mortals.— Look to it, that, in this, ye offend not.

It is further enjoined that ye take strict charge of this book; that no one but the priests do touch it with their hands, and that it be preserved in a chest of alabaster, to be placed under the altar in the midst of the temple. It is in like way commanded that copies of the book be written as occasion requireth, and that they be transmitted unto the priest of the other temples throughout the earth: also that they be deposited in the tombs of the KINGS and of the HIGH PRIESTS, as followeth:—

When the body hath been embalmed and sufficiently swathed in fine cloth, let the roll of writing be place under the left breast, and let the vestment be bound over it, so that it shall be covered close and hid from view. The body shall then be attended by the princes and priests and people to the place of sepulture, where it is to be interred with honour;—a strong and durable building being raised on the top thereof.

How the Enquirer shall obtain a True Answer to the Question which he putteth to the Oracle

When a man or woman doth come to enquire ought of you, O Priests! let the gifts be made and the sacrifices offered up; and let the invocations of the servants of the temple be chaunted.

When silence hath been restored, The DIVINER shall direct the stranger who hath come to enquire of the ORACLE, to trace, with a reed dipped in the blood of the sacrifice, in the midst of a circle containing the twelve SIGNS OF THE ZODIAC,* five rows of upright or inclined lines, taking care that each be readily seen to contain more than twelve lines, in respect of the number of the SIGNS OF THE ZODIAC, but he must by no means do this studiously, or count the number he hath marked, but guide the reed quickly, so that the number, while it be more than twelve, shall be entirely of chance, as far as he knoweth.

The DIVINER shall now reckon from the left unto the right hand line of each row, which the inquirer hath written, marking off twelve, thus:

$$||||||||||||,|||$$

and keeping count of the remainder, so that he may know whether the remaining number of each be odd or even.

If the number of a row be odd, the DIVINER shall attach to the right hand side thereof one small star, and if it be even, he shall attach two stars; and in the same manner with other rows, as herein set down:—

This double column of stars shall be, to the DIVINER, for a SIGN whereby he shall be enabled to discover the fate of the ENQUIRER.

Let the ENQUIRER now consult his own breast what he requireth to know; and whether the matter cometh within compass of the questions herein writ, and set down in order, as followeth.** — If it doth, the ENQUIRER shall straightaway pronounce the

---

* The translator feels it incumbent on him, here to notice (from the experience of himself and others in consulting the Oracle), that he considers some of the above mentioned formalities may, on most occasions, be dispensed with. He has found that for all ordinary consultations the circle and signs may be omitted; and instead of a reed dipped in blood, he and his friends have, invariably and without the least detriment, used a pen dipped in common ink. As to the gifts, sacrifices, and invocations, he considers them in a Christian land to be entirely superfluous; but in their stead it is doubtless requisite that the consulter should have a firm reliance on the goodness and providence of the Creator of all things.

** See the Frontispiece, containing the questions, their hieroglyphics and signs.

question, audibly, as it is written, without adding to, or diminishing therefrom, and shall, while he uttereth the words, point to the number of the question with the forefinger of his left hand.

The DIVINER, in his proper vestments, having invoked OSIRIS, shall now place the forefinger of his right hand on the spot whereon the ENQUIRER had previously placed the same finger of his left. He shall then search out among the SIGNS, or columns of stars, placed above the hieroglyphics, for that individual SIGN, or column, which shall answer in every respect to the one which hath been cast up, by the addition of the lines previously traced by the ENQUIRER.

When the DIVINER hath found the corresponding SIGN, or column of stars, he must place thereon the forefinger of his left hand; he shall now move this finger, and likewise the same finger of the right hand, from the points whereon they have been placed, so that they may approximate, or meet each other, at right angles.

The HIEROGLYPHIC whereat the fingers meet, must now be noted; and the DIVINER, having looked into the roll, is therein to search out the counterpart of the same HIEROGLYPHIC.

Having found it, he is to search further on the left hand side of the matter, or answers, appended unto this hieroglyphic, for the counterpart of the SIGN, or column of stars, which, in the commencement of the consultation, had incidentally, or BY THE ORDINATION OF FATE, been produced by the enumeration of the surplus over twelve of the lines traced by the ENQUIRER within the circle.

The words attached to the SIGN, or column of stars, will be the just and true answer to the question put; which see no one do pervert to any false purpose of deceit, enmity or wickedness.

No further ceremony now remaineth, but that the PRIEST who hath acted in the divination, do write down the answer truly, and, with his finger placed upon his lips, hand it unto the PROPHET or PROPHETESS, who shall in a loud voice proclaim its contents unto the person who came to enquire.*

---

\* In order to make the English reader, as much as possible, acquainted with the proper mode of finding answers to the questions of those who consult the Oracle, it will be necessary here to state one example. I shall take the same rows of lines, and the same SIGN, or double column of stars, as are set down in the original instructions for consultation, as above. We shall suppose, then, that the QUESTION asked is No. 27, as marked in the Frontispiece or TABLE, viz:—Shall my intended journey be prosperous or unlucky? By looking at the column of stars, or SIGN, corresponding with that cast up, we shall find it numbered 20, and the consequent HIEROGLYPHIC produced by the combination of this SIGN and the QUESTION asked, will be that of the CROSS BONES. Now by reference to this HIEROGLYPHIC and its subservient SIGN, or column of stars, in the Book of Fate, we find that the

In conclusion, I am commanded to write unto you, that it is the duty of the PRIESTS to instruct all those who consult the ORACLE, that it behoveth them to be contented with whatever ANSWER they may, through FATE, receive; and to follow implicitly, and without reservation, whatever the ORACLE, in its ANSWERS, may happen to dictate. If the instructions of HERMES be not obeyed, what booteth it to enquire?—If the CONSULTER be herein disobedient to the will of OSIRIS, the evil be upon his own head.

Further, O PRIESTS! be warned to make no divination, nor to admit of any gift, sacrifice or consultation, save during the night season, and that, too, only whilst ISIS shineth in the fullness of her beauty.* Neither shall ye give ANSWERS on those days or nights in which either OSIRIS who ruleth the heavens by day, or the Queen of his love, who ruleth by night, do veil the comeliness and majesty of their countenances from the eyes of mortals, and whilst they do retire from the labours of their celestial course, within the chambers of their sanctuary of rest.**

These are the word which I, BALASPIS, have been commanded, by my great master HERMES TRISMEGISTUS, to write unto you, O PRIESTS OF THEBAIS.

---

ANSWER given by the Oracle is 'When thou hast arrived at thy place of destination, lose no time in executing thy errand, and return without delay,' which ANSWER, whilst it suggests a necessary caution, whereby evil or danger is avoided, perfectly corresponds with the QUESTION asked.

In a similar way, appropriate ANSWERS will be given to all the other QUESTIONS in the TABLE; that is, by paying attention to their particular HIEROGLYPHICS and SIGNS.

N.B. The Translator considers it proper to state, that in order to facilitate the search for the Hieroglyphic (resulting from the combination of the QUESTION and SIGNS) in the BOOK OF FATE, it will be proper for the CONSULTER to cast his eye over the highest line of Hieroglyphics in the FRONTISPIECE, and note the NUMBER which lies immediately over it. This number will be found to correspond with that folio of the BOOK OF FATE, over which presides the Hieroglyphic in question.


* I presume that here the meaning of BALASPIS is, that the Oracle should not be consulted but when the MOON is at the full. Among the ancient Egyptians ISIS typified the Moon, whilst the name of OSIRIS was always given to the Sun.

** By this mode of expression, it is evident that eclipses of the SUN and MOON are meant: But it is necessary to notice that, as far as the experience of the translator and his friends has enabled them to judge, there is no apparent reason or necessity for confining the consultation of the Oracle to any particular time or season. One thing, however, the Consulter should be aware of, which is, that it would be improper for him to ask two questions on the same day; or even to ask the same questions, with reference to the same subject, twice within one calendar month.

QUESTIONS which may be put to the ORACLE and which
will be truly answered according to the HIEROGLYPHICAL
INDICATIONS of the PLANETS.

1   Inform me of any or of all particulars which relate to
    the Woman I shall Marry?

2   Will the Prisoner be released or continue captive?

3   Shall I live to an Old Age?

4   Shall I have to travel far by Sea or Land, or to reside in
    foreign Climes?

5   Shall I be involved in Litigation & if so, shall I gain or
    lose my Cause?

6   Shall I make, or mar, my Fortune by Gambling?

7   Shall I ever be able to retire from business, with a
    Fortune?

8   Shall I be eminent and meet with Preferment in my
    Pursuits?

9   Shall I be Successful in my present undertaking?

10  Shall I ever inherit Testamentary property?

11  Shall I spend this Year Happier than the last?

12  Will my Name be Immortalized & will posterity
    applaud it?

13  Will the friend, I most reckon upon, prove faithful or
    treacherous?

14  Will the stolen Property be recovered & will the Thief
    be detected?

15  What is the aspect of the Seasons & what Political
    Changes are likely to take place?

16  Will the Stranger soon return from abroad?

17  Will my Beloved prove true in my absence?

18  Will the Marriage about to take place be happy and
    prosperous?

19  After my death will my Children be virtuous & happy?

20   Shall I ever recover from my present Misfortune?

21   Does my Dream portend good luck or Misfortune?

22   Will it be my lot to experience great Vicissitudes in this Life?

23   Will my reputation be at all, or much, affected by Calumny?

24   Inform me of all particulars relating to my future Husband?

25   Shall the Patient recover from Illness?

26   Does the person whom I love Love and regard me?

27   Shall my intended Journey be prosperous or unlucky?

28   Shall I ever find a Treasure?

29   What Trade, or Profession, ought I to follow?

30   Have I any, or many, Enemies?

31   Are Absent Friends in good health & what is their present employment?

32   Shall my Wife have a Son or a Daughter?

**1** Inform me of any or of all particulars which relate to the Woman I shall Marry?

| | | | |
|---|---|---|---|
| ★<br>★<br>★ = 1<br>★<br>★ | ★<br>★<br>★ ★ = 265<br>★ ★<br>★ | ★ ★<br>★ ★<br>★ ★ = 529<br>★<br>★ | ★ ★<br>★ ★<br>★ = 793<br>★ ★<br>★ |
| ★ ★<br>★<br>★ = 34<br>★<br>★ | ★<br>★<br>★ = 298<br>★ ★<br>★ ★ | ★<br>★ ★<br>★ ★ = 562<br>★ ★<br>★ | ★ ★<br>★<br>★ ★ = 826<br>★ ★<br>★ |
| ★<br>★ ★<br>★ = 67<br>★<br>★ | ★<br>★<br>★ ★ = 331<br>★<br>★ ★ | ★<br>★<br>★ ★ = 595<br>★ ★<br>★ ★ | ★ ★<br>★ ★<br>★ ★ = 859<br>★ ★<br>★ |
| ★<br>★<br>★ ★ = 100<br>★<br>★ | ★<br>★ ★<br>★ = 364<br>★ ★<br>★ | ★<br>★ ★<br>★ = 628<br>★ ★<br>★ ★ | ★ ★<br>★<br>★ ★ = 892<br>★ ★<br>★ ★ |
| ★<br>★<br>★ = 133<br>★ ★<br>★ | ★ ★<br>★<br>★ ★ = 397<br>★<br>★ | ★<br>★ ★<br>★ ★ = 661<br>★<br>★ ★ | ★ ★<br>★ ★<br>★ = 925<br>★ ★<br>★ ★ |
| ★<br>★<br>★ = 166<br>★<br>★ ★ | ★<br>★ ★<br>★ = 430<br>★<br>★ ★ | ★ ★<br>★<br>★ = 694<br>★ ★<br>★ ★ | ★ ★<br>★ ★<br>★ ★ = 958<br>★<br>★ ★ |
| ★ ★<br>★ ★<br>★ = 199<br>★<br>★ | ★ ★<br>★<br>★ = 463<br>★ ★<br>★ | ★ ★<br>★<br>★ ★ = 727<br>★<br>★ ★ | ★<br>★ ★<br>★ ★ = 991<br>★ ★<br>★ ★ |
| ★<br>★ ★<br>★ ★ = 232<br>★<br>★ | ★ ★<br>★<br>★ = 496<br>★<br>★ ★ | ★ ★<br>★ ★<br>★ = 760<br>★<br>★ ★ | ★ ★<br>★ ★<br>★ ★ = 1024<br>★ ★<br>★ ★ |

## 2 Will the **Prisoner** be released or continue captive?

| | | | |
|---|---|---|---|
| ★<br>★<br>★ = 33<br>★<br>★ | ★<br>★<br>★ ★ = 297<br>★ ★<br>★ | ★ ★<br>★ ★<br>★ ★ = 561<br>★<br>★ | ★ ★<br>★ ★<br>★ = 825<br>★ ★<br>★ |
| ★ ★<br>★<br>★ = 66<br>★<br>★ | ★<br>★ = 330<br>★ ★<br>★ ★ | ★<br>★ ★<br>★ ★ = 594<br>★ ★<br>★ | ★ ★<br>★ = 858<br>★ ★<br>★ |
| ★<br>★ ★<br>★ = 99<br>★<br>★ | ★<br>★<br>★ ★ = 363<br>★<br>★ ★ | ★<br>★<br>★ ★ = 627<br>★ ★<br>★ ★ | ★ ★<br>★ ★<br>★ ★ = 891<br>★ ★<br>★ |
| ★<br>★<br>★ ★ = 132<br>★<br>★ | ★<br>★ ★<br>★ = 396<br>★ ★<br>★ | ★<br>★ ★<br>★ = 660<br>★ ★<br>★ ★ | ★ ★<br>★<br>★ ★ = 924<br>★ ★<br>★ ★ |
| ★<br>★<br>★ = 165<br>★ ★<br>★ | ★ ★<br>★<br>★ ★ = 429<br>★<br>★ | ★<br>★ ★<br>★ ★ = 693<br>★<br>★ ★ | ★ ★<br>★ ★<br>★ = 957<br>★ ★<br>★ ★ |
| ★<br>★<br>★ = 198<br>★<br>★ ★ | ★<br>★ ★<br>★ = 462<br>★<br>★ ★ | ★ ★<br>★<br>★ = 726<br>★ ★<br>★ ★ | ★ ★<br>★ ★<br>★ = 990<br>★<br>★ ★ |
| ★ ★<br>★ ★<br>★ = 231<br>★<br>★ | ★ ★<br>★<br>★ = 495<br>★ ★<br>★ | ★ ★<br>★<br>★ ★ = 759<br>★<br>★ ★ | ★<br>★ ★<br>★ ★ = 1023<br>★ ★<br>★ ★ |
| ★<br>★ ★<br>★ ★ = 264<br>★<br>★ | ★ ★<br>★<br>★ = 528<br>★<br>★ ★ | ★ ★<br>★ ★<br>★ = 792<br>★<br>★ ★ | ★ ★<br>★ ★<br>★ ★ = 32<br>★ ★<br>★ ★ |

## 3   Shall I live to an **Old Age?**

| | | | |
|---|---|---|---|
| ★<br>★<br>★ = 65<br>★<br>★ | ★<br>★<br>★ ★ = 329<br>★ ★<br>★ | ★ ★<br>★ ★<br>★ ★ = 593<br>★<br>★ | ★ ★<br>★ ★<br>★ = 857<br>★ ★<br>★ |
| ★ ★<br>★<br>★ = 98<br>★<br>★ | ★<br>★<br>★ = 362<br>★ ★<br>★ ★ | ★<br>★ ★<br>★ ★ = 626<br>★ ★<br>★ | ★ ★<br>★<br>★ ★ = 890<br>★ ★<br>★ |
| ★<br>★ ★<br>★ = 131<br>★<br>★ | ★<br>★<br>★ ★ = 395<br>★<br>★ ★ | ★<br>★<br>★ ★ = 659<br>★ ★<br>★ ★ | ★ ★<br>★ ★<br>★ ★ = 923<br>★ ★<br>★ |
| ★<br>★<br>★ ★ = 164<br>★<br>★ | ★<br>★ ★<br>★ = 428<br>★ ★<br>★ | ★<br>★ ★<br>★ = 692<br>★ ★<br>★ ★ | ★ ★<br>★<br>★ ★ = 956<br>★ ★<br>★ ★ |
| ★<br>★<br>★ = 197<br>★ ★<br>★ | ★ ★<br>★<br>★ ★ = 461<br>★<br>★ | ★<br>★ ★<br>★ ★ = 725<br>★<br>★ ★ | ★ ★<br>★ ★<br>★ = 989<br>★ ★<br>★ ★ |
| ★<br>★<br>★ = 230<br>★<br>★ ★ | ★<br>★ ★<br>★ = 494<br>★<br>★ ★ | ★ ★<br>★<br>★ = 758<br>★ ★<br>★ ★ | ★ ★<br>★ ★<br>★ ★ = 1022<br>★<br>★ ★ |
| ★ ★<br>★ ★<br>★ = 263<br>★<br>★ | ★<br>★ ★<br>★ = 527<br>★ ★<br>★ | ★ ★<br>★<br>★ ★ = 791<br>★<br>★ ★ | ★<br>★ ★<br>★ ★ = 31<br>★ ★<br>★ ★ |
| ★<br>★ ★<br>★ ★ = 296<br>★<br>★ | ★ ★<br>★<br>★ = 560<br>★<br>★ ★ | ★ ★<br>★ ★<br>★ = 824<br>★<br>★ ★ | ★ ★<br>★ ★<br>★ ★ = 64<br>★ ★<br>★ ★ |

## 4 Shall I have to travel far by Sea or Land, or to reside in foreign Climes?

| | | | |
|---|---|---|---|
| ★<br>★<br>★ = 97<br>★<br>★ | ★<br>★<br>★★ = 361<br>★★<br>★ | ★★<br>★★<br>★★ = 625<br>★<br>★ | ★★<br>★★<br>★ = 889<br>★★<br>★ |
| ★★<br>★<br>★ = 130<br>★<br>★ | ★<br>★<br>★ = 394<br>★★<br>★★ | ★<br>★★<br>★★ = 658<br>★★<br>★ | ★★<br>★<br>★★ = 922<br>★★<br>★ |
| ★<br>★★<br>★ = 163<br>★<br>★ | ★<br>★<br>★★ = 427<br>★<br>★★ | ★<br>★<br>★★ = 691<br>★★<br>★★ | ★★<br>★★<br>★★ = 955<br>★★<br>★ |
| ★<br>★<br>★★ = 196<br>★<br>★ | ★<br>★★<br>★ = 460<br>★★<br>★ | ★<br>★★<br>★ = 724<br>★★<br>★★ | ★★<br>★<br>★★ = 988<br>★★<br>★★ |
| ★<br>★<br>★ = 229<br>★★<br>★ | ★★<br>★<br>★★ = 493<br>★<br>★ | ★★<br>★★<br>★ = 757<br>★<br>★★ | ★★<br>★★<br>★ = 1021<br>★★<br>★★ |
| ★<br>★<br>★ = 262<br>★<br>★★ | ★<br>★★<br>★ = 526<br>★<br>★★ | ★★<br>★<br>★ = 790<br>★★<br>★★ | ★★<br>★★<br>★★ = 30<br>★<br>★★ |
| ★★<br>★★<br>★ = 295<br>★<br>★ | ★★<br>★<br>★ = 559<br>★★<br>★ | ★★<br>★<br>★★ = 823<br>★<br>★★ | ★<br>★★<br>★★ = 63<br>★★<br>★★ |
| ★<br>★★<br>★★ = 328<br>★<br>★ | ★★<br>★<br>★ = 592<br>★<br>★★ | ★★<br>★★<br>★ = 856<br>★<br>★★ | ★★<br>★★<br>★★ = 96<br>★★<br>★★ |

## 5 Shall I be involved in **Litigation** & if so, shall I gain or lose my Cause?

| | | | |
|---|---|---|---|
| ★<br>★<br>★ = 129<br>★<br>★ | ★<br>★<br>★ ★ = 393<br>★ ★<br>★ | ★ ★<br>★ ★<br>★ ★ = 657<br>★<br>★ | ★ ★<br>★ ★<br>★ = 921<br>★ ★<br>★ |
| ★ ★<br>★<br>★ = 162<br>★<br>★ | ★<br>★<br>★ = 426<br>★ ★<br>★ ★ | ★<br>★ ★<br>★ ★ = 690<br>★ ★<br>★ | ★ ★<br>★<br>★ ★ = 954<br>★ ★<br>★ |
| ★<br>★ ★<br>★ = 195<br>★<br>★ | ★<br>★<br>★ ★ = 459<br>★<br>★ ★ | ★<br>★<br>★ ★ = 723<br>★ ★<br>★ ★ | ★ ★<br>★ ★<br>★ ★ = 987<br>★ ★<br>★ |
| ★<br>★<br>★ ★ = 228<br>★<br>★ | ★<br>★ ★<br>★ = 492<br>★ ★<br>★ | ★<br>★ ★<br>★ = 756<br>★ ★<br>★ ★ | ★ ★<br>★<br>★ ★ = 1020<br>★ ★<br>★ ★ |
| ★<br>★<br>★ = 261<br>★ ★<br>★ | ★ ★<br>★<br>★ ★ = 525<br>★<br>★ | ★<br>★ ★<br>★ ★ = 789<br>★<br>★ ★ | ★ ★<br>★ ★<br>★ = 29<br>★ ★<br>★ ★ |
| ★<br>★<br>★ = 294<br>★<br>★ ★ | ★<br>★ ★<br>★ = 558<br>★<br>★ ★ | ★ ★<br>★<br>★ = 822<br>★ ★<br>★ ★ | ★ ★<br>★ ★<br>★ = 62<br>★<br>★ ★ |
| ★ ★<br>★ ★<br>★ = 327<br>★<br>★ | ★<br>★ ★<br>★ = 591<br>★ ★<br>★ | ★ ★<br>★<br>★ ★ = 855<br>★<br>★ ★ | ★<br>★ ★<br>★ ★ = 95<br>★ ★<br>★ ★ |
| ★<br>★ ★<br>★ ★ = 360<br>★<br>★ | ★ ★<br>★<br>★ = 624<br>★<br>★ ★ | ★ ★<br>★ ★<br>★ = 888<br>★<br>★ ★ | ★ ★<br>★ ★<br>★ ★ = 128<br>★ ★<br>★ ★ |

## 6 Shall I make, or mar, my Fortune by **Gambling?**

| | | | |
|---|---|---|---|
| ★ ★ ★ ★ ★ = 161 | ★ ★ ★★ ★★ ★ = 425 | ★★ ★★ ★★ ★ ★ = 689 | ★★ ★★ ★ ★★ ★ = 953 |
| ★★ ★ ★ ★ ★ = 194 | ★ ★ ★ ★★ ★★ = 458 | ★ ★★ ★★ ★ = 722 | ★★ ★ ★★ ★★ ★ = 986 |
| ★ ★★ ★ ★ ★ = 227 | ★ ★ ★★ ★ ★★ = 491 | ★ ★ ★★ ★★ = 755 | ★★ ★★ ★★ ★★ ★ = 1019 |
| ★ ★ ★★ ★ ★ = 260 | ★ ★★ ★ ★★ ★ = 524 | ★ ★★ ★ ★★ ★★ = 788 | ★★ ★ ★★ ★★ ★★ = 28 |
| ★ ★ ★ ★★ ★ = 293 | ★★ ★ ★★ ★ ★ = 557 | ★ ★★ ★★ ★ ★★ = 821 | ★★ ★★ ★ ★★ ★★ = 61 |
| ★ ★ ★ ★ ★★ = 326 | ★★ ★ ★ ★ ★★ = 590 | ★ ★ ★★ ★★ = 854 | ★★ ★★ ★★ ★ ★★ = 94 |
| ★★ ★★ ★ ★ ★ = 359 | ★★ ★ ★ ★★ ★ = 623 | ★★ ★ ★★ ★ ★★ = 887 | ★ ★★ ★★ ★★ ★★ = 127 |
| ★ ★★ ★★ ★ ★ = 392 | ★★ ★ ★ ★ ★★ = 656 | ★★ ★★ ★ ★ ★★ = 920 | ★★ ★★ ★★ ★★ ★★ = 160 |

## 7 Shall I ever be able to retire from business with a Fortune?

| | | | |
|---|---|---|---|
| ★<br>★<br>★ = 193<br>★<br>★ | ★<br>★<br>★ ★ = 457<br>★ ★<br>★ | ★ ★<br>★ ★<br>★ ★ = 721<br>★<br>★ | ★ ★<br>★ ★<br>★ = 985<br>★ ★<br>★ |
| ★ ★<br>★<br>★ = 226<br>★<br>★ | ★<br>★<br>★ = 490<br>★ ★<br>★ ★ | ★<br>★ ★<br>★ ★ = 754<br>★ ★<br>★ | ★ ★<br>★<br>★ ★ = 1018<br>★ ★<br>★ |
| ★<br>★ ★<br>★ = 259<br>★<br>★ | ★<br>★<br>★ ★ = 523<br>★<br>★ ★ | ★<br>★<br>★ ★ = 787<br>★ ★<br>★ ★ | ★ ★<br>★ ★<br>★ ★ = 27<br>★ ★<br>★ |
| ★<br>★<br>★ ★ = 292<br>★<br>★ | ★<br>★ ★<br>★ = 556<br>★ ★<br>★ | ★<br>★ ★<br>★ = 820<br>★ ★<br>★ ★ | ★ ★<br>★<br>★ ★ = 60<br>★ ★<br>★ ★ |
| ★<br>★<br>★ = 325<br>★ ★<br>★ | ★ ★<br>★<br>★ ★ = 589<br>★<br>★ | ★<br>★ ★<br>★ ★ = 853<br>★<br>★ ★ | ★ ★<br>★ ★<br>★ = 93<br>★ ★<br>★ ★ |
| ★<br>★<br>★ = 358<br>★<br>★ ★ | ★<br>★ ★<br>★ = 622<br>★<br>★ ★ | ★ ★<br>★<br>★ = 886<br>★ ★<br>★ ★ | ★ ★<br>★ ★<br>★ ★ = 126<br>★<br>★ ★ |
| ★ ★<br>★ ★<br>★ = 391<br>★<br>★ | ★ ★<br>★<br>★ = 655<br>★ ★<br>★ | ★ ★<br>★<br>★ ★ = 919<br>★<br>★ ★ | ★<br>★ ★<br>★ ★ = 159<br>★ ★<br>★ ★ |
| ★<br>★ ★<br>★ ★ = 424<br>★<br>★ | ★ ★<br>★<br>★ = 688<br>★<br>★ ★ | ★ ★<br>★ ★<br>★ = 952<br>★<br>★ ★ | ★ ★<br>★ ★<br>★ ★ = 192<br>★ ★<br>★ ★ |

## 8 Shall I be eminent and meet with **Preferment** in my Pursuits?

| | | | |
|---|---|---|---|
| ★<br>★<br>★ = 225<br>★<br>★ | ★<br>★<br>★ ★ = 489<br>★ ★<br>★ | ★ ★<br>★ ★<br>★ ★ = 753<br>★<br>★ | ★ ★<br>★ ★<br>★ = 1017<br>★ ★<br>★ |
| ★ ★<br>★<br>★ = 258<br>★<br>★ | ★<br>★<br>★ = 522<br>★ ★<br>★ ★ | ★<br>★ ★<br>★ ★ = 786<br>★ ★<br>★ | ★ ★<br>★<br>★ ★ = 26<br>★ ★<br>★ |
| ★<br>★ ★<br>★ = 291<br>★<br>★ | ★<br>★<br>★ ★ = 555<br>★<br>★ ★ | ★<br>★<br>★ ★ = 819<br>★ ★<br>★ ★ | ★ ★<br>★ ★<br>★ ★ = 59<br>★ ★<br>★ |
| ★<br>★<br>★ ★ = 324<br>★<br>★ | ★<br>★ ★<br>★ = 588<br>★ ★<br>★ | ★<br>★ ★<br>★ = 852<br>★ ★<br>★ ★ | ★ ★<br>★<br>★ ★ = 92<br>★ ★<br>★ ★ |
| ★<br>★<br>★ = 357<br>★ ★<br>★ | ★ ★<br>★<br>★ ★ = 621<br>★<br>★ | ★<br>★ ★<br>★ ★ = 885<br>★<br>★ ★ | ★ ★<br>★ ★<br>★ = 125<br>★ ★<br>★ ★ |
| ★<br>★<br>★ = 390<br>★<br>★ ★ | ★<br>★ ★<br>★ = 654<br>★<br>★ ★ | ★<br>★<br>★ = 918<br>★ ★<br>★ ★ | ★ ★<br>★ ★<br>★ ★ = 158<br>★<br>★ ★ |
| ★ ★<br>★ ★<br>★ = 423<br>★<br>★ | ★ ★<br>★<br>★ = 687<br>★ ★<br>★ | ★ ★<br>★<br>★ ★ = 951<br>★<br>★ ★ | ★<br>★ ★<br>★ ★ = 191<br>★ ★<br>★ ★ |
| ★<br>★ ★<br>★ ★ = 456<br>★<br>★ | ★ ★<br>★<br>★ = 720<br>★<br>★ ★ | ★ ★<br>★ ★<br>★ = 984<br>★<br>★ ★ | ★ ★<br>★ ★<br>★ ★ = 224<br>★ ★<br>★ ★ |

## 9  Shall I be **Successful** in my present undertaking?

| | | | |
|---|---|---|---|
| ★<br>★<br>★ = 257<br>★<br>★ | ★<br>★<br>★ ★ = 521<br>★ ★<br>★ | ★ ★<br>★ ★<br>★ ★ = 785<br>★<br>★ | ★ ★<br>★ ★<br>★ = 25<br>★ ★<br>★ |
| ★ ★<br>★<br>★ = 290<br>★<br>★ | ★<br>★<br>★ = 554<br>★ ★<br>★ ★ | ★<br>★ ★<br>★ ★ = 818<br>★ ★<br>★ | ★ ★<br>★<br>★ ★ = 58<br>★ ★<br>★ |
| ★<br>★ ★<br>★ = 323<br>★<br>★ | ★<br>★<br>★ ★ = 587<br>★<br>★ ★ | ★<br>★<br>★ ★ = 851<br>★ ★<br>★ ★ | ★ ★<br>★ ★<br>★ ★ = 91<br>★ ★<br>★ |
| ★<br>★<br>★ ★ = 356<br>★<br>★ | ★<br>★ ★<br>★ = 620<br>★ ★<br>★ | ★<br>★ ★<br>★ = 884<br>★ ★<br>★ ★ | ★ ★<br>★<br>★ ★ = 124<br>★ ★<br>★ ★ |
| ★<br>★<br>★ = 389<br>★ ★<br>★ | ★ ★<br>★<br>★ ★ = 653<br>★<br>★ | ★<br>★ ★<br>★ ★ = 917<br>★<br>★ ★ | ★ ★<br>★ ★<br>★ = 157<br>★ ★<br>★ ★ |
| ★<br>★<br>★ = 422<br>★<br>★ ★ | ★<br>★ ★<br>★ = 686<br>★<br>★ ★ | ★ ★<br>★<br>★ = 950<br>★ ★<br>★ ★ | ★ ★<br>★ ★<br>★ ★ = 190<br>★<br>★ ★ |
| ★ ★<br>★ ★<br>★ = 455<br>★<br>★ | ★ ★<br>★<br>★ = 719<br>★ ★<br>★ | ★ ★<br>★<br>★ ★ = 983<br>★<br>★ ★ | ★<br>★ ★<br>★ ★ = 223<br>★ ★<br>★ ★ |
| ★<br>★ ★<br>★ ★ = 488<br>★<br>★ | ★ ★<br>★<br>★ = 752<br>★<br>★ ★ | ★ ★<br>★ ★<br>★ = 1016<br>★<br>★ ★ | ★ ★<br>★ ★<br>★ ★ = 256<br>★ ★<br>★ ★ |

# 10   Shall I ever inherit **Testamentary** property?

| | | | |
|---|---|---|---|
| ★ ★ ★ ★ ★ = 289 | ★ ★ ★★ ★★ ★ = 553 | ★★ ★★ ★★ ★ ★ = 817 | ★★ ★★ ★ ★★ ★ = 57 |
| ★★ ★ ★ ★ = 322 | ★ ★ ★ ★★ ★★ = 586 | ★ ★★ ★★ ★★ ★ = 850 | ★★ ★ ★★ ★★ ★ = 90 |
| ★ ★★ ★ ★ ★ = 355 | ★ ★ ★ ★ ★★ = 619 | ★ ★ ★★ ★★ ★★ = 883 | ★★ ★★ ★★ ★★ ★ = 123 |
| ★ ★ ★★ ★ ★ = 388 | ★ ★★ ★ ★★ ★ = 652 | ★ ★★ ★ ★★ ★★ = 916 | ★★ ★ ★★ ★★ ★★ = 156 |
| ★ ★ ★ ★★ ★ = 421 | ★★ ★ ★★ ★ ★ = 685 | ★ ★★ ★★ ★ ★★ = 949 | ★★ ★★ ★ ★★ ★★ = 189 |
| ★ ★ ★ ★ ★★ = 454 | ★★ ★ ★ ★★ = 718 | ★ ★ ★★ ★★ = 982 | ★★ ★★ ★★ ★ ★★ = 222 |
| ★★ ★★ ★ ★ ★ = 487 | ★★ ★ ★ ★★ ★ = 751 | ★★ ★ ★★ ★ ★★ = 1015 | ★ ★★ ★★ ★★ ★★ = 255 |
| ★ ★★ ★★ ★ ★ = 520 | ★★ ★ ★ ★ ★★ = 784 | ★★ ★★ ★ ★ ★★ = 24 | ★★ ★★ ★★ ★★ = 288 |

## 11  Shall I spend this Year **Happier** than the last?

| | | | |
|---|---|---|---|
| ★<br>★<br>★ = 321<br>★<br>★ | ★<br>★<br>★ ★ = 585<br>★ ★<br>★ | ★ ★<br>★ ★<br>★ ★ = 849<br>★<br>★ | ★ ★<br>★ ★<br>★ = 89<br>★ ★<br>★ |
| ★ ★<br>★<br>★ = 354<br>★<br>★ | ★<br>★<br>★ = 618<br>★ ★<br>★ ★ | ★<br>★ ★<br>★ ★ = 882<br>★ ★<br>★ | ★ ★<br>★<br>★ ★ = 122<br>★ ★<br>★ |
| ★<br>★ ★<br>★ = 387<br>★<br>★ | ★<br>★<br>★ ★ = 651<br>★<br>★ ★ | ★<br>★<br>★ ★ = 915<br>★ ★<br>★ ★ | ★ ★<br>★ ★<br>★ ★ = 155<br>★ ★<br>★ |
| ★<br>★<br>★ ★ = 420<br>★<br>★ | ★<br>★ ★<br>★ = 684<br>★ ★<br>★ | ★<br>★ ★<br>★ = 948<br>★ ★<br>★ ★ | ★ ★<br>★<br>★ ★ = 188<br>★ ★<br>★ ★ |
| ★<br>★<br>★ = 453<br>★ ★<br>★ | ★ ★<br>★<br>★ ★ = 717<br>★<br>★ | ★<br>★ ★<br>★ ★ = 981<br>★<br>★ ★ | ★ ★<br>★ ★<br>★ = 221<br>★ ★<br>★ ★ |
| ★<br>★<br>★ = 486<br>★<br>★ ★ | ★<br>★ ★<br>★ = 750<br>★<br>★ ★ | ★ ★<br>★<br>★ = 1014<br>★ ★<br>★ ★ | ★ ★<br>★ ★<br>★ = 254<br>★<br>★ ★ |
| ★ ★<br>★ ★<br>★ = 519<br>★<br>★ | ★ ★<br>★<br>★ = 783<br>★ ★<br>★ | ★ ★<br>★<br>★ ★ = 23<br>★<br>★ ★ | ★<br>★ ★<br>★ ★ = 287<br>★ ★<br>★ ★ |
| ★<br>★ ★<br>★ ★ = 552<br>★<br>★ | ★ ★<br>★<br>★ = 816<br>★<br>★ ★ | ★ ★<br>★ ★<br>★ = 56<br>★<br>★ ★ | ★ ★<br>★ ★<br>★ ★ = 320<br>★ ★<br>★ ★ |

| | | | |
|---|---|---|---|
| **12** Will my **Name** be **Immortalized** & will posterity applaud it? | | | |
| ★<br>★<br>★ = 353<br>★<br>★ | ★<br>★<br>★ ★ = 617<br>★ ★<br>★ | ★ ★<br>★ ★<br>★ ★ = 881<br>★<br>★ | ★ ★<br>★ ★<br>★ = 121<br>★ ★<br>★ |
| ★ ★<br>★<br>★ = 386<br>★<br>★ | ★<br>★<br>★ = 650<br>★ ★<br>★ ★ | ★<br>★ ★<br>★ ★ = 914<br>★ ★<br>★ | ★ ★<br>★<br>★ ★ = 154<br>★ ★<br>★ |
| ★<br>★ ★<br>★ = 419<br>★<br>★ | ★<br>★<br>★ ★ = 683<br>★<br>★ ★ | ★<br>★<br>★ ★ = 946<br>★ ★<br>★ ★ | ★ ★<br>★ ★<br>★ ★ = 187<br>★ ★<br>★ |
| ★<br>★<br>★ ★ = 452<br>★<br>★ | ★<br>★ ★<br>★ = 716<br>★ ★<br>★ | ★<br>★ ★<br>★ = 980<br>★ ★<br>★ ★ | ★ ★<br>★<br>★ ★ = 220<br>★ ★<br>★ ★ |
| ★<br>★<br>★ = 485<br>★ ★<br>★ | ★ ★<br>★<br>★ ★ = 749<br>★<br>★ | ★<br>★ ★<br>★ ★ = 1013<br>★<br>★ ★ | ★ ★<br>★ ★<br>★ = 253<br>★ ★<br>★ ★ |
| ★<br>★<br>★ = 518<br>★<br>★ ★ | ★<br>★ ★<br>★ = 782<br>★<br>★ ★ | ★ ★<br>★<br>★ = 22<br>★ ★<br>★ ★ | ★ ★<br>★ ★<br>★ ★ = 286<br>★<br>★ ★ |
| ★ ★<br>★ ★<br>★ = 551<br>★<br>★ | ★ ★<br>★<br>★ = 815<br>★ ★<br>★ | ★ ★<br>★<br>★ ★ = 55<br>★<br>★ ★ | ★<br>★ ★<br>★ ★ = 319<br>★ ★<br>★ ★ |
| ★<br>★ ★<br>★ ★ = 584<br>★<br>★ | ★ ★<br>★<br>★ = 848<br>★<br>★ ★ | ★ ★<br>★ ★<br>★ = 88<br>★<br>★ ★ | ★ ★<br>★ ★<br>★ ★ = 352<br>★ ★<br>★ ★ |

**13** Will the **Friend**, I most reckon upon, prove faithful or treacherous?

| | | | |
|---|---|---|---|
| ★<br>★<br>★ = 385<br>★<br>★ | ★<br>★<br>★★ = 649<br>★★<br>★ | ★★<br>★★<br>★★ = 913<br>★<br>★ | ★★<br>★★<br>★ = 153<br>★★<br>★ |
| ★★<br>★<br>★ = 418<br>★<br>★ | ★<br>★<br>★ = 682<br>★★<br>★★ | ★<br>★★<br>★★ = 947<br>★★<br>★ | ★★<br>★<br>★★ = 186<br>★★<br>★ |
| ★<br>★★<br>★ = 451<br>★<br>★ | ★<br>★<br>★★ = 715<br>★<br>★★ | ★<br>★<br>★★ = 979<br>★★<br>★★ | ★★<br>★★<br>★★ = 219<br>★★<br>★ |
| ★<br>★<br>★★ = 484<br>★<br>★ | ★<br>★★<br>★ = 748<br>★★<br>★ | ★<br>★★<br>★ = 1012<br>★★<br>★★ | ★★<br>★<br>★★ = 252<br>★★<br>★★ |
| ★<br>★<br>★ = 517<br>★★<br>★ | ★★<br>★★<br>★ = 781<br>★<br>★ | ★<br>★★<br>★★ = 21<br>★<br>★★ | ★★<br>★★<br>★ = 285<br>★★<br>★★ |
| ★<br>★<br>★ = 550<br>★<br>★★ | ★★<br>★★<br>★ = 814<br>★<br>★★ | ★★<br>★<br>★ = 54<br>★★<br>★★ | ★★<br>★★<br>★ = 318<br>★<br>★★ |
| ★★<br>★★<br>★ = 583<br>★<br>★ | ★★<br>★<br>★ = 847<br>★★<br>★ | ★★<br>★<br>★★ = 87<br>★<br>★★ | ★<br>★★<br>★★ = 351<br>★★<br>★★ |
| ★<br>★★<br>★★ = 616<br>★<br>★ | ★★<br>★<br>★ = 880<br>★<br>★★ | ★★<br>★★<br>★ = 120<br>★<br>★★ | ★★<br>★★<br>★★ = 384<br>★★<br>★★ |

| 14 Will the stolen **Property** be recovered & will the **Thief** be detected? | | | |
|---|---|---|---|
| ★<br>★<br>★ = 417<br>★<br>★ | ★<br>★<br>★ ★ = 681<br>★ ★<br>★ | ★ ★<br>★ ★<br>★ ★ = 945<br>★<br>★ | ★ ★<br>★ ★<br>★ = 185<br>★ ★<br>★ |
| ★ ★<br>★ = 450<br>★<br>★ | ★<br>★<br>★ = 714<br>★ ★<br>★ ★ | ★<br>★ ★<br>★ ★ = 978<br>★ ★<br>★ | ★ ★<br>★<br>★ ★ = 218<br>★ ★<br>★ |
| ★<br>★ ★<br>★ = 483<br>★<br>★ | ★<br>★<br>★ ★ = 747<br>★<br>★ ★ | ★<br>★<br>★ ★ = 1011<br>★ ★<br>★ ★ | ★ ★<br>★ ★<br>★ ★ = 251<br>★ ★<br>★ |
| ★<br>★<br>★ ★ = 516<br>★<br>★ | ★<br>★ ★<br>★ = 780<br>★ ★<br>★ | ★<br>★ ★<br>★ = 20<br>★ ★<br>★ ★ | ★ ★<br>★<br>★ ★ = 284<br>★ ★<br>★ ★ |
| ★<br>★<br>★ = 549<br>★ ★<br>★ | ★ ★<br>★<br>★ ★ = 813<br>★<br>★ | ★<br>★ ★<br>★ ★ = 53<br>★<br>★ ★ | ★ ★<br>★ ★<br>★ = 317<br>★ ★<br>★ ★ |
| ★<br>★<br>★ = 582<br>★<br>★ ★ | ★<br>★ ★<br>★ = 846<br>★<br>★ ★ | ★ ★<br>★<br>★ = 86<br>★ ★<br>★ ★ | ★ ★<br>★ ★<br>★ ★ = 350<br>★<br>★ ★ |
| ★ ★<br>★ ★<br>★ = 615<br>★<br>★ | ★ ★<br>★<br>★ = 879<br>★ ★<br>★ | ★ ★<br>★<br>★ ★ = 119<br>★<br>★ ★ | ★<br>★ ★<br>★ ★ = 383<br>★ ★<br>★ ★ |
| ★<br>★ ★<br>★ ★ = 648<br>★<br>★ | ★ ★<br>★<br>★ = 912<br>★<br>★ ★ | ★ ★<br>★ ★<br>★ = 152<br>★<br>★ ★ | ★ ★<br>★ ★<br>★ ★ = 416<br>★ ★<br>★ ★ |

## 15 What are the aspect of the **Seasons** & what **Political Changes** are likely to take place?

| | | | |
|---|---|---|---|
| ★<br>★<br>★ = 449<br>★<br>★ | ★<br>★<br>★★ = 713<br>★★<br>★ | ★★<br>★★<br>★★ = 977<br>★<br>★ | ★★<br>★★<br>★ = 217<br>★★<br>★ |
| ★★<br>★<br>★ = 482<br>★<br>★ | ★<br>★<br>★ = 746<br>★★<br>★★ | ★<br>★★<br>★★ = 1010<br>★★<br>★ | ★★<br>★<br>★★ = 250<br>★★<br>★ |
| ★<br>★★<br>★ = 515<br>★<br>★ | ★<br>★<br>★★ = 779<br>★<br>★★ | ★<br>★<br>★★ = 19<br>★★<br>★★ | ★★<br>★★<br>★★ = 283<br>★★<br>★ |
| ★<br>★<br>★★ = 548<br>★<br>★ | ★<br>★★<br>★ = 812<br>★★<br>★ | ★<br>★★<br>★ = 52<br>★★<br>★★ | ★★<br>★<br>★★ = 316<br>★★<br>★★ |
| ★<br>★<br>★ = 581<br>★★<br>★ | ★★<br>★<br>★★ = 845<br>★<br>★ | ★<br>★★<br>★★ = 85<br>★<br>★★ | ★★<br>★★<br>★ = 349<br>★★<br>★★ |
| ★<br>★<br>★ = 614<br>★<br>★★ | ★<br>★★<br>★ = 878<br>★<br>★★ | ★★<br>★<br>★ = 118<br>★★<br>★★ | ★★<br>★★<br>★★ = 382<br>★<br>★★ |
| ★★<br>★★<br>★ = 647<br>★<br>★ | ★★<br>★<br>★ = 911<br>★★<br>★ | ★★<br>★<br>★ = 151<br>★<br>★★ | ★<br>★★<br>★★ = 415<br>★★<br>★★ |
| ★<br>★★<br>★★ = 680<br>★<br>★ | ★★<br>★<br>★ = 944<br>★<br>★★ | ★★<br>★★<br>★ = 184<br>★<br>★★ | ★★<br>★★<br>★★ = 448<br>★★<br>★★ |

| **16** | Will the **Stranger** soon return from abroad? | | |
|---|---|---|---|
| ★<br>★<br>★ = 481<br>★<br>★ | ★<br>★<br>★ ★ = 745<br>★ ★<br>★ | ★ ★<br>★ ★<br>★ ★ = 1009<br>★<br>★ | ★ ★<br>★ ★<br>★ = 249<br>★ ★<br>★ |
| ★ ★<br>★ = 514<br>★<br>★ | ★<br>★<br>★ = 778<br>★ ★<br>★ ★ | ★<br>★ ★<br>★ ★ = 18<br>★ ★<br>★ | ★ ★<br>★<br>★ ★ = 282<br>★ ★<br>★ |
| ★<br>★ ★<br>★ = 547<br>★<br>★ | ★<br>★<br>★ ★ = 811<br>★<br>★ ★ | ★<br>★<br>★ ★ = 51<br>★ ★<br>★ ★ | ★ ★<br>★ ★<br>★ ★ = 315<br>★ ★<br>★ |
| ★<br>★<br>★ ★ = 580<br>★<br>★ | ★<br>★ ★<br>★ = 844<br>★ ★<br>★ | ★<br>★ ★<br>★ = 84<br>★ ★<br>★ ★ | ★ ★<br>★<br>★ ★ = 348<br>★ ★<br>★ ★ |
| ★<br>★<br>★ = 613<br>★ ★<br>★ | ★ ★<br>★<br>★ ★ = 877<br>★<br>★ | ★<br>★ ★<br>★ ★ = 117<br>★<br>★ ★ | ★ ★<br>★ ★<br>★ = 381<br>★ ★<br>★ ★ |
| ★<br>★<br>★ = 646<br>★<br>★ ★ | ★<br>★ ★<br>★ = 910<br>★<br>★ ★ | ★ ★<br>★ = 150<br>★ ★<br>★ ★ | ★ ★<br>★ ★<br>★ ★ = 414<br>★<br>★ ★ |
| ★ ★<br>★ ★<br>★ = 679<br>★<br>★ | ★<br>★<br>★ = 943<br>★ ★<br>★ | ★ ★<br>★<br>★ ★ = 183<br>★<br>★ ★ | ★<br>★ ★<br>★ ★ = 447<br>★ ★<br>★ ★ |
| ★<br>★ ★<br>★ ★ = 712<br>★<br>★ | ★ ★<br>★<br>★ = 976<br>★<br>★ ★ | ★ ★<br>★ ★<br>★ = 216<br>★<br>★ ★ | ★ ★<br>★ ★<br>★ ★ = 480<br>★ ★<br>★ ★ |

## 17   Will my **Beloved** prove true in my absence?

| | | | |
|---|---|---|---|
| = 513 | = 777 | = 17 | = 281 |
| = 546 | = 810 | = 50 | = 314 |
| = 579 | = 843 | = 83 | = 347 |
| = 612 | = 876 | = 116 | = 380 |
| = 645 | = 909 | = 149 | = 413 |
| = 678 | = 942 | = 182 | = 446 |
| = 711 | = 975 | = 215 | = 479 |
| = 744 | = 1008 | = 248 | = 512 |

| 18 | Will the **Marriage** about to take place be happy and prosperous? | | |
|---|---|---|---|
| ★<br>★<br>★ = **545**<br>★<br>★ | ★<br>★<br>★★ = **809**<br>★★<br>★ | ★★<br>★★<br>★★ = **49**<br>★<br>★ | ★★<br>★★<br>★ = **313**<br>★★<br>★ |
| ★★<br>★<br>★ = **578**<br>★<br>★ | ★<br>★<br>★ = **842**<br>★★<br>★★ | ★<br>★★<br>★★ = **82**<br>★★<br>★ | ★★<br>★<br>★★ = **346**<br>★★<br>★ |
| ★<br>★★<br>★ = **611**<br>★<br>★ | ★<br>★<br>★★ = **875**<br>★<br>★★ | ★<br>★<br>★★ = **115**<br>★★<br>★★ | ★★<br>★★<br>★★ = **379**<br>★★<br>★ |
| ★<br>★<br>★★ = **644**<br>★<br>★ | ★<br>★★<br>★ = **908**<br>★★<br>★ | ★<br>★★<br>★ = **148**<br>★★<br>★★ | ★★<br>★<br>★★ = **412**<br>★★<br>★★ |
| ★<br>★<br>★ = **677**<br>★★<br>★ | ★★<br>★<br>★★ = **941**<br>★<br>★ | ★<br>★★<br>★★ = **181**<br>★<br>★★ | ★★<br>★★<br>★ = **445**<br>★★<br>★★ |
| ★<br>★<br>★ = **710**<br>★<br>★★ | ★★<br>★<br>★ = **974**<br>★<br>★★ | ★★<br>★ = **214**<br>★★<br>★★ | ★★<br>★★<br>★ = **478**<br>★<br>★★ |
| ★★<br>★★<br>★ = **743**<br>★<br>★ | ★★<br>★ = **1007**<br>★★<br>★ | ★★<br>★<br>★★ = **247**<br>★<br>★★ | ★<br>★★<br>★★ = **511**<br>★★<br>★★ |
| ★<br>★★<br>★★ = **776**<br>★<br>★ | ★★<br>★<br>★ = **16**<br>★<br>★★ | ★★<br>★★<br>★ = **280**<br>★<br>★★ | ★★<br>★★<br>★★ = **544**<br>★★<br>★★ |

**19** After my death will my **Children** be virtuous & happy?

| | | | |
|---|---|---|---|
| ★<br>★<br>★ = **577**<br>★<br>★ | ★<br>★<br>★ ★ = **841**<br>★ ★<br>★ | ★ ★<br>★ ★<br>★ ★ = **81**<br>★<br>★ | ★ ★<br>★ ★<br>★ = **345**<br>★ ★<br>★ |
| ★ ★<br>★<br>★ = **610**<br>★<br>★ | ★<br>★<br>★ ★ = **874**<br>★ ★<br>★ ★ | ★<br>★ ★<br>★ ★ = **114**<br>★ ★<br>★ | ★ ★<br>★<br>★ ★ = **378**<br>★ ★<br>★ |
| ★<br>★ ★<br>★ = **643**<br>★<br>★ | ★<br>★<br>★ ★ = **907**<br>★<br>★ ★ | ★<br>★<br>★ ★ = **147**<br>★ ★<br>★ ★ | ★ ★<br>★ ★<br>★ ★ = **411**<br>★ ★<br>★ |
| ★<br>★<br>★ ★ = **676**<br>★<br>★ | ★<br>★ ★<br>★ = **940**<br>★ ★<br>★ | ★<br>★ ★<br>★ = **180**<br>★ ★<br>★ ★ | ★ ★<br>★<br>★ ★ = **444**<br>★ ★<br>★ ★ |
| ★<br>★<br>★ = **709**<br>★ ★<br>★ | ★ ★<br>★<br>★ ★ = **973**<br>★<br>★ | ★<br>★ ★<br>★ ★ = **213**<br>★<br>★ ★ | ★ ★<br>★ ★<br>★ = **477**<br>★ ★<br>★ ★ |
| ★<br>★<br>★ = **742**<br>★<br>★ ★ | ★<br>★ ★<br>★ = **1006**<br>★<br>★ ★ | ★ ★<br>★<br>★ = **246**<br>★ ★<br>★ ★ | ★ ★<br>★ ★<br>★ ★ = **510**<br>★<br>★ ★ |
| ★ ★<br>★ ★<br>★ = **775**<br>★<br>★ | ★ ★<br>★<br>★ = **15**<br>★ ★<br>★ | ★ ★<br>★<br>★ ★ = **279**<br>★<br>★ ★ | ★<br>★ ★<br>★ ★ = **543**<br>★ ★<br>★ ★ |
| ★<br>★ ★<br>★ ★ = **808**<br>★<br>★ | ★ ★<br>★<br>★ = **48**<br>★<br>★ ★ | ★ ★<br>★ ★<br>★ = **312**<br>★<br>★ ★ | ★ ★<br>★ ★<br>★ ★ = **576**<br>★ ★<br>★ ★ |

# 20 Shall I ever recover from my present **Misfortune**?

| | | | |
|---|---|---|---|
| ★<br>★<br>★ = 609<br>★<br>★ | ★<br>★ ★ = 873<br>★ ★ | ★ ★<br>★ ★<br>★ ★ = 113<br>★<br>★ | ★ ★<br>★ ★<br>★ = 377<br>★ ★<br>★ |
| ★ ★<br>★<br>★ = 642<br>★<br>★ | ★<br>★ = 906<br>★ ★<br>★ ★ | ★<br>★ ★<br>★ ★ = 146<br>★ ★<br>★ | ★ ★<br>★<br>★ ★ = 410<br>★ ★<br>★ |
| ★<br>★ ★<br>★ = 675<br>★<br>★ | ★<br>★<br>★ = 939<br>★<br>★ ★ | ★<br>★<br>★ ★ = 179<br>★ ★<br>★ ★ | ★ ★<br>★ ★<br>★ ★ = 443<br>★ ★<br>★ |
| ★<br>★<br>★ ★ = 708<br>★<br>★ | ★<br>★ ★<br>★ = 972<br>★ ★<br>★ | ★<br>★ ★<br>★ = 212<br>★ ★<br>★ ★ | ★ ★<br>★<br>★ ★ = 476<br>★ ★<br>★ ★ |
| ★<br>★<br>★ = 741<br>★ ★<br>★ | ★ ★<br>★ ★ = 1005<br>★<br>★ | ★<br>★ ★<br>★ ★ = 245<br>★<br>★ ★ | ★ ★<br>★ ★<br>★ = 509<br>★ ★<br>★ ★ |
| ★<br>★<br>★ = 774<br>★<br>★ ★ | ★<br>★ ★ = 14<br>★<br>★ ★ | ★ ★<br>★ = 278<br>★ ★<br>★ ★ | ★ ★<br>★ ★<br>★ ★ = 542<br>★<br>★ ★ |
| ★ ★<br>★ ★<br>★ = 807<br>★<br>★ | ★ ★<br>★ = 47<br>★ ★<br>★ | ★ ★<br>★<br>★ ★ = 311<br>★<br>★ ★ | ★<br>★ ★<br>★ ★ = 575<br>★ ★<br>★ ★ |
| ★<br>★ ★<br>★ ★ = 840<br>★<br>★ | ★ ★<br>★ = 80<br>★<br>★ ★ | ★ ★<br>★ ★<br>★ = 344<br>★<br>★ ★ | ★ ★<br>★ ★<br>★ ★ = 608<br>★ ★<br>★ ★ |

## 21   Does my **Dream** portend good luck or Misfortune?

| | | | |
|---|---|---|---|
| ★<br>★<br>★ = **641**<br>★<br>★ | ★<br>★<br>★★ = **905**<br>★★<br>★ | ★★<br>★★<br>★★ = **145**<br>★<br>★ | ★★<br>★★<br> ★ = **409**<br>★★<br>★ |
| ★★<br>★<br>★ = **674**<br>★<br>★ | ★<br>★<br>★ = **938**<br>★★<br>★★ | ★<br>★★<br>★★ = **178**<br>★★<br>★ | ★★<br>★<br>★★ = **442**<br>★★<br>★ |
| ★<br>★★<br>★ = **707**<br>★<br>★ | ★<br>★<br>★★ = **971**<br>★<br>★★ | ★<br>★<br>★★ = **211**<br>★★<br>★★ | ★★<br>★★<br>★★ = **475**<br>★★<br>★ |
| ★<br>★<br>★★ = **740**<br>★<br>★ | ★<br>★★<br>★ = **1004**<br>★★<br>★ | ★<br>★★<br>★ = **244**<br>★★<br>★★ | ★★<br>★<br>★★ = **508**<br>★★<br>★★ |
| ★<br>★<br>★ = **773**<br>★★<br>★ | ★★<br>★<br>★★ = **13**<br>★<br>★ | ★<br>★★<br>★★ = **277**<br>★<br>★★ | ★★<br>★★<br>★ = **541**<br>★★<br>★★ |
| ★<br>★<br>★ = **806**<br>★<br>★★ | ★<br>★★<br>★ = **46**<br>★<br>★★ | ★★<br>★<br>★ = **310**<br>★★<br>★★ | ★★<br>★★<br>★★ = **574**<br>★<br>★★ |
| ★★<br>★★<br>★ = **839**<br>★<br>★ | ★★<br>★<br>★ = **79**<br>★★<br>★ | ★★<br>★<br>★★ = **343**<br>★<br>★★ | ★<br>★★<br>★★ = **607**<br>★★<br>★★ |
| ★<br>★★<br>★★ = **872**<br>★<br>★ | ★★<br>★<br>★ = **112**<br>★<br>★★ | ★★<br>★★<br>★ = **376**<br>★<br>★★ | ★★<br>★★<br>★★ = **640**<br>★★<br>★★ |

| | | | |
|---|---|---|---|
| **22** Will it be my lot to experience great **Vicissitudes** in this Life? | | | |

| | | | |
|---|---|---|---|
| ★<br>★<br>★ = 673<br>★<br>★ | ★<br>★<br>★ ★ = 937<br>★ ★<br>★ | ★ ★<br>★ ★<br>★ ★ = 177<br>★<br>★ | ★ ★<br>★ ★<br>★ = 441<br>★ ★<br>★ |
| ★ ★<br>★<br>★ = 706<br>★<br>★ | ★<br>★<br>★ = 970<br>★ ★<br>★ ★ | ★<br>★ ★<br>★ ★ = 210<br>★ ★<br>★ | ★ ★<br>★<br>★ ★ = 474<br>★ ★<br>★ |
| ★<br>★ ★<br>★ = 739<br>★<br>★ | ★<br>★<br>★ ★ = 1003<br>★<br>★ ★ | ★<br>★<br>★ ★ = 243<br>★ ★<br>★ ★ | ★ ★<br>★ ★<br>★ ★ = 507<br>★ ★<br>★ |
| ★<br>★<br>★ ★ = 772<br>★<br>★ | ★<br>★ ★<br>★ = 12<br>★ ★<br>★ | ★<br>★ ★<br>★ = 276<br>★ ★<br>★ ★ | ★ ★<br>★<br>★ ★ = 540<br>★ ★<br>★ ★ |
| ★<br>★<br>★ = 805<br>★ ★<br>★ | ★ ★<br>★<br>★ ★ = 45<br>★<br>★ | ★<br>★ ★<br>★ ★ = 309<br>★<br>★ ★ | ★ ★<br>★ ★<br>★ = 573<br>★ ★<br>★ ★ |
| ★<br>★<br>★ = 838<br>★<br>★ ★ | ★<br>★ ★<br>★ = 78<br>★<br>★ ★ | ★ ★<br>★<br>★ = 342<br>★ ★<br>★ ★ | ★ ★<br>★ ★<br>★ ★ = 606<br>★<br>★ ★ |
| ★ ★<br>★ ★<br>★ = 871<br>★<br>★ | ★ ★<br>★<br>★ = 111<br>★ ★<br>★ | ★ ★<br>★<br>★ ★ = 375<br>★<br>★ ★ | ★<br>★ ★<br>★ ★ = 639<br>★ ★<br>★ ★ |
| ★<br>★ ★<br>★ ★ = 904<br>★<br>★ | ★ ★<br>★<br>★ = 144<br>★<br>★ ★ | ★ ★<br>★ ★<br>★ = 408<br>★<br>★ ★ | ★ ★<br>★ ★<br>★ ★ = 672<br>★ ★<br>★ ★ |

## 23. Will my reputation be at all or much affected by Calumny?

| | | | |
|---|---|---|---|
| ★ ★ ★ ★ ★ = **705** | ★ ★ ★★ ★★ ★ = **969** | ★★ ★★ ★★ ★ ★ = **209** | ★★ ★★ ★ ★★ ★ = **473** |
| ★★ ★ ★ ★ ★ = **738** | ★ ★ ★ ★★ ★★ = **1002** | ★ ★★ ★★ ★★ ★ = **242** | ★★ ★ ★★ ★★ ★ = **506** |
| ★ ★★ ★ ★ ★ = **771** | ★ ★ ★★ ★ ★★ = **11** | ★ ★ ★★ ★★ ★★ = **275** | ★★ ★★ ★★ ★★ ★ = **539** |
| ★ ★ ★★ ★ ★ = **804** | ★ ★★ ★ ★★ ★ = **44** | ★ ★★ ★ ★★ ★★ = **308** | ★★ ★ ★★ ★★ ★★ = **572** |
| ★ ★ ★ ★★ ★ = **837** | ★★ ★ ★★ ★ ★ = **77** | ★ ★★ ★★ ★ ★★ = **341** | ★★ ★★ ★ ★★ ★★ = **605** |
| ★ ★ ★ ★ ★★ = **870** | ★ ★★ ★ ★ ★★ = **110** | ★★ ★ ★★ ★★ = **374** | ★★ ★★ ★★ ★ ★★ = **638** |
| ★★ ★★ ★ ★ ★ = **903** | ★★ ★ ★ ★★ ★ = **143** | ★★ ★ ★★ ★ ★★ = **407** | ★ ★★ ★★ ★★ ★★ = **671** |
| ★ ★★ ★★ ★ ★ = **936** | ★★ ★ ★ ★ ★★ = **176** | ★★ ★★ ★ ★ ★★ = **440** | ★★ ★★ ★★ ★★ ★★ = **704** |

## 24. Inform me of all particulars relating to my future Husband?

| | | | |
|---|---|---|---|
| ★<br>★<br>★ = 737<br>★<br>★ | ★<br>★<br>★ ★ = 1001<br>★ ★<br>★ | ★ ★<br>★ ★<br>★ ★ = 241<br>★<br>★ | ★ ★<br>★ ★<br>★ = 505<br>★ ★<br>★ |
| ★ ★<br>★<br>★ = 770<br>★<br>★ | ★<br>★<br>★ = 10<br>★ ★<br>★ ★ | ★<br>★ ★<br>★ ★ = 274<br>★ ★<br>★ | ★ ★<br>★<br>★ ★ = 538<br>★ ★<br>★ |
| ★<br>★ ★<br>★ = 803<br>★<br>★ | ★<br>★<br>★ ★ = 43<br>★<br>★ ★ | ★<br>★<br>★ ★ = 307<br>★ ★<br>★ ★ | ★ ★<br>★ ★<br>★ ★ = 571<br>★ ★<br>★ |
| ★<br>★<br>★ ★ = 836<br>★<br>★ | ★<br>★ ★<br>★ = 76<br>★ ★<br>★ | ★<br>★ ★<br>★ = 340<br>★ ★<br>★ ★ | ★ ★<br>★<br>★ ★ = 604<br>★ ★<br>★ ★ |
| ★<br>★<br>★ = 869<br>★ ★<br>★ | ★ ★<br>★<br>★ ★ = 109<br>★<br>★ | ★<br>★ ★<br>★ ★ = 373<br>★<br>★ ★ | ★ ★<br>★ ★<br>★ = 637<br>★ ★<br>★ ★ |
| ★<br>★<br>★ = 902<br>★<br>★ ★ | ★<br>★ ★<br>★ = 142<br>★<br>★ ★ | ★ ★<br>★<br>★ = 406<br>★ ★<br>★ ★ | ★ ★<br>★ ★<br>★ ★ = 670<br>★<br>★ ★ |
| ★ ★<br>★ ★<br>★ = 935<br>★<br>★ | ★<br>★<br>★ = 175<br>★ ★<br>★ | ★ ★<br>★<br>★ ★ = 439<br>★<br>★ ★ | ★<br>★ ★<br>★ ★ = 703<br>★ ★<br>★ ★ |
| ★<br>★ ★<br>★ ★ = 968<br>★<br>★ | ★ ★<br>★<br>★ = 208<br>★<br>★ ★ | ★ ★<br>★ ★<br>★ = 472<br>★<br>★ ★ | ★ ★<br>★ ★<br>★ ★ = 736<br>★ ★<br>★ ★ |

## 25 Shall the **Patient** recover from Illness?

| | | | |
|---|---|---|---|
| ★<br>★<br>★ = **769**<br>★<br>★ | ★<br>★<br>★ ★ = **9**<br>★ ★<br>★ | ★ ★<br>★ ★<br>★ ★ = **273**<br>★<br>★ | ★ ★<br>★ ★<br>★ = **537**<br>★ ★<br>★ |
| ★ ★<br>★<br>★ = **802**<br>★<br>★ | ★<br>★<br>★ = **42**<br>★ ★<br>★ ★ | ★<br>★ ★<br>★ ★ = **306**<br>★ ★<br>★ | ★ ★<br>★<br>★ ★ = **570**<br>★ ★<br>★ |
| ★<br>★ ★<br>★ = **835**<br>★<br>★ | ★<br>★<br>★ ★ = **75**<br>★<br>★ ★ | ★<br>★<br>★ ★ = **339**<br>★ ★<br>★ ★ | ★ ★<br>★ ★<br>★ ★ = **603**<br>★ ★<br>★ |
| ★<br>★<br>★ ★ = **868**<br>★<br>★ | ★<br>★ ★<br>★ = **108**<br>★ ★<br>★ | ★<br>★ ★<br>★ = **372**<br>★ ★<br>★ ★ | ★ ★<br>★<br>★ ★ = **636**<br>★ ★<br>★ ★ |
| ★<br>★<br>★ = **901**<br>★ ★<br>★ | ★ ★<br>★ ★ = **141**<br>★<br>★ | ★<br>★ ★<br>★ ★ = **405**<br>★<br>★ ★ | ★ ★<br>★ ★<br>★ = **669**<br>★ ★<br>★ ★ |
| ★<br>★<br>★ = **934**<br>★<br>★ ★ | ★<br>★ ★<br>★ = **174**<br>★<br>★ ★ | ★ ★<br>★<br>★ = **438**<br>★ ★<br>★ ★ | ★ ★<br>★ ★<br>★ ★ = **702**<br>★<br>★ ★ |
| ★ ★<br>★ ★<br>★ = **967**<br>★<br>★ | ★ ★<br>★<br>★ = **207**<br>★ ★<br>★ | ★ ★<br>★<br>★ ★ = **471**<br>★<br>★ ★ | ★<br>★ ★<br>★ ★ = **735**<br>★ ★<br>★ ★ |
| ★<br>★ ★<br>★ ★ = **1000**<br>★<br>★ | ★ ★<br>★<br>★ = **240**<br>★<br>★ ★ | ★ ★<br>★ ★<br>★ = **504**<br>★<br>★ ★ | ★ ★<br>★ ★<br>★ ★ = **768**<br>★ ★<br>★ ★ |

## 26 Does the person whom I love Love and regard me?

| | | | |
|---|---|---|---|
| ★<br>★<br>★ = 801<br>★<br>★ | ★<br>★<br>★ ★ = 41<br>★ ★<br>★ | ★ ★<br>★ ★<br>★ ★ = 305<br>★<br>★ | ★ ★<br>★ ★<br>★ = 569<br>★ ★<br>★ |
| ★ ★<br>★<br>★ = 834<br>★<br>★ | ★<br>★<br>★ = 74<br>★ ★<br>★ ★ | ★<br>★ ★<br>★ ★ = 338<br>★ ★<br>★ | ★ ★<br>★<br>★ ★ = 602<br>★ ★<br>★ |
| ★<br>★ ★<br>★ = 867<br>★<br>★ | ★<br>★<br>★ ★ = 107<br>★<br>★ ★ | ★<br>★<br>★ ★ = 371<br>★ ★<br>★ ★ | ★ ★<br>★ ★<br>★ ★ = 635<br>★ ★<br>★ |
| ★<br>★<br>★ ★ = 900<br>★<br>★ | ★<br>★ ★<br>★ = 140<br>★ ★<br>★ | ★<br>★ ★<br>★ = 404<br>★ ★<br>★ ★ | ★ ★<br>★<br>★ ★ = 668<br>★ ★<br>★ ★ |
| ★<br>★<br>★ = 933<br>★ ★<br>★ | ★ ★<br>★<br>★ ★ = 173<br>★<br>★ | ★<br>★ ★<br>★ ★ = 437<br>★<br>★ ★ | ★ ★<br>★ ★<br>★ = 701<br>★ ★<br>★ ★ |
| ★<br>★<br>★ = 966<br>★<br>★ ★ | ★<br>★ ★<br>★ = 206<br>★<br>★ ★ | ★ ★<br>★<br>★ = 470<br>★ ★<br>★ ★ | ★ ★<br>★ ★<br>★ ★ = 734<br>★<br>★ ★ |
| ★ ★<br>★ ★<br>★ = 999<br>★<br>★ | ★ ★<br>★<br>★ = 239<br>★ ★<br>★ | ★ ★<br>★<br>★ ★ = 503<br>★<br>★ ★ | ★<br>★ ★<br>★ ★ = 767<br>★ ★<br>★ ★ |
| ★<br>★ ★<br>★ ★ = 8<br>★<br>★ | ★ ★<br>★<br>★ = 272<br>★<br>★ ★ | ★ ★<br>★ ★<br>★ = 536<br>★<br>★ ★ | ★ ★<br>★ ★<br>★ ★ = 800<br>★ ★<br>★ ★ |

## 27 Shall my intended **Journey** be prosperous or unlucky?

| | | | |
|---|---|---|---|
| ★<br>★<br>★ = 833<br>★<br>★ | ★<br>★<br>★ ★ = 73<br>★ ★<br>★ | ★ ★<br>★ ★<br>★ ★ = 337<br>★<br>★ | ★ ★<br>★ ★<br>★ = 601<br>★ ★<br>★ |
| ★ ★<br>★<br>★ = 866<br>★<br>★ | ★<br>★<br>★ = 106<br>★ ★<br>★ ★ | ★<br>★ ★<br>★ ★ = 370<br>★ ★<br>★ | ★ ★<br>★<br>★ ★ = 634<br>★ ★<br>★ |
| ★<br>★ ★<br>★ = 899<br>★<br>★ | ★<br>★<br>★ ★ = 139<br>★<br>★ ★ | ★<br>★<br>★ ★ = 403<br>★ ★<br>★ ★ | ★ ★<br>★ ★<br>★ ★ = 667<br>★ ★<br>★ |
| ★<br>★<br>★ ★ = 932<br>★<br>★ | ★<br>★ ★<br>★ = 172<br>★ ★<br>★ | ★<br>★ ★<br>★ = 436<br>★ ★<br>★ ★ | ★ ★<br>★<br>★ ★ = 700<br>★ ★<br>★ ★ |
| ★<br>★<br>★ = 965<br>★ ★<br>★ | ★ ★<br>★<br>★ ★ = 205<br>★<br>★ | ★<br>★ ★<br>★ ★ = 469<br>★<br>★ ★ | ★ ★<br>★ ★<br>★ = 733<br>★ ★<br>★ ★ |
| ★<br>★<br>★ = 998<br>★<br>★ ★ | ★<br>★ ★<br>★ = 238<br>★<br>★ ★ | ★ ★<br>★<br>★ = 502<br>★ ★<br>★ ★ | ★ ★<br>★ ★<br>★ ★ = 766<br>★<br>★ ★ |
| ★ ★<br>★ ★<br>★ = 7<br>★<br>★ | ★<br>★ ★<br>★ = 271<br>★ ★<br>★ | ★ ★<br>★<br>★ ★ = 535<br>★<br>★ ★ | ★<br>★ ★<br>★ ★ = 799<br>★ ★<br>★ ★ |
| ★<br>★ ★<br>★ ★ = 40<br>★<br>★ | ★ ★<br>★<br>★ = 304<br>★<br>★ ★ | ★ ★<br>★ ★<br>★ = 568<br>★<br>★ ★ | ★ ★<br>★ ★<br>★ ★ = 832<br>★ ★<br>★ ★ |

# 28 Shall I ever find a **Treasure**?

| | | | |
|---|---|---|---|
| ★<br>★<br>★ = 865<br>★<br>★ | ★<br>★<br>★★ = 105<br>★★<br>★ | ★★<br>★★<br>★★ = 369<br>★<br>★ | ★★<br>★★<br>★ = 633<br>★★<br>★ |
| ★★<br>★<br>★ = 898<br>★<br>★ | ★<br>★<br>★ = 138<br>★★<br>★★ | ★<br>★★<br>★★ = 402<br>★★<br>★ | ★★<br>★<br>★★ = 666<br>★★<br>★ |
| ★<br>★★<br>★ = 931<br>★<br>★ | ★<br>★<br>★★ = 171<br>★<br>★★ | ★<br>★<br>★★ = 435<br>★★<br>★★ | ★★<br>★★<br>★★ = 699<br>★★<br>★ |
| ★<br>★<br>★★ = 964<br>★<br>★ | ★<br>★★<br>★ = 204<br>★★<br>★ | ★<br>★★<br>★ = 468<br>★★<br>★★ | ★★<br>★<br>★★ = 732<br>★★<br>★★ |
| ★<br>★<br>★ = 997<br>★★<br>★ | ★★<br>★<br>★★ = 237<br>★<br>★ | ★<br>★★<br>★★ = 501<br>★<br>★★ | ★★<br>★★<br>★ = 765<br>★★<br>★★ |
| ★<br>★<br>★ = 6<br>★<br>★★ | ★<br>★★<br>★ = 270<br>★<br>★★ | ★★<br>★<br>★ = 534<br>★★<br>★★ | ★★<br>★★<br>★★ = 798<br>★<br>★★ |
| ★★<br>★★<br>★ = 39<br>★<br>★ | ★★<br>★<br>★ = 303<br>★★<br>★ | ★★<br>★<br>★★ = 567<br>★<br>★★ | ★<br>★★<br>★★ = 831<br>★★<br>★★ |
| ★<br>★★<br>★★ = 72<br>★<br>★ | ★★<br>★<br>★ = 336<br>★<br>★★ | ★★<br>★★<br>★ = 600<br>★<br>★★ | ★★<br>★★<br>★★ = 864<br>★★<br>★★ |

## 29 What **Trade**, or **Profession**, ought I to follow?

| ★ pattern = | ★ pattern = | ★ pattern = | ★ pattern = |
|---|---|---|---|
| = 897 | = 137 | = 401 | = 665 |
| = 930 | = 170 | = 434 | = 698 |
| = 963 | = 203 | = 467 | = 731 |
| = 996 | = 236 | = 500 | = 764 |
| = 5 | = 269 | = 533 | = 797 |
| = 38 | = 302 | = 566 | = 830 |
| = 71 | = 335 | = 599 | = 863 |
| = 104 | = 368 | = 632 | = 896 |

## 30 Have I any, or many, **Enemies?**

| | | | |
|---|---|---|---|
| ★<br>★<br>★ = 929<br>★<br>★ | ★<br>★<br>★ ★ = 169<br>★ ★<br>★ | ★ ★<br>★ ★<br>★ ★ = 433<br>★<br>★ | ★ ★<br>★ ★<br>★ = 697<br>★ ★<br>★ |
| ★ ★<br>★<br>★ = 962<br>★<br>★ | ★<br>★<br>★ = 202<br>★ ★<br>★ ★ | ★<br>★ ★<br>★ ★ = 466<br>★ ★<br>★ | ★ ★<br>★<br>★ ★ = 730<br>★ ★<br>★ |
| ★<br>★ ★<br>★ = 995<br>★<br>★ | ★<br>★<br>★ ★ = 235<br>★<br>★ ★ | ★<br>★<br>★ ★ = 499<br>★ ★<br>★ ★ | ★ ★<br>★ ★<br>★ ★ = 763<br>★ ★<br>★ |
| ★<br>★<br>★ ★ = 4<br>★<br>★ | ★<br>★ ★<br>★ = 268<br>★ ★<br>★ | ★<br>★ ★<br>★ = 532<br>★ ★<br>★ ★ | ★ ★<br>★<br>★ ★ = 796<br>★ ★<br>★ ★ |
| ★<br>★<br>★ = 37<br>★ ★<br>★ | ★ ★<br>★<br>★ ★ = 301<br>★<br>★ | ★<br>★ ★<br>★ ★ = 565<br>★<br>★ ★ | ★ ★<br>★ ★<br>★ = 829<br>★ ★<br>★ ★ |
| ★<br>★<br>★ = 70<br>★<br>★ ★ | ★<br>★ ★<br>★ = 334<br>★<br>★ ★ | ★ ★<br>★<br>★ = 598<br>★ ★<br>★ ★ | ★ ★<br>★ ★<br>★ ★ = 862<br>★<br>★ ★ |
| ★ ★<br>★ ★<br>★ = 103<br>★<br>★ | ★ ★<br>★<br>★ = 367<br>★ ★<br>★ | ★ ★<br>★<br>★ ★ = 631<br>★<br>★ ★ | ★<br>★ ★<br>★ ★ = 895<br>★ ★<br>★ ★ |
| ★<br>★ ★<br>★ ★ = 136<br>★<br>★ | ★ ★<br>★<br>★ = 400<br>★<br>★ ★ | ★ ★<br>★ ★<br>★ = 664<br>★<br>★ ★ | ★ ★<br>★ ★<br>★ ★ = 928<br>★ ★<br>★ ★ |

## 31  Are **Absent Friends** in good health & what is their present employment?

| | | | |
|---|---|---|---|
| ★<br>★<br>★ = **961**<br>★<br>★ | ★<br>★<br>★★ = **201**<br>★★<br>★ | ★★<br>★★<br>★★ = **465**<br>★<br>★ | ★★<br>★★<br>★ = **729**<br>★★<br>★ |
| ★★<br>★<br>★ = **994**<br>★<br>★ | ★<br>★<br>★ = **234**<br>★★<br>★★ | ★<br>★★<br>★★ = **498**<br>★★<br>★ | ★★<br>★<br>★★ = **762**<br>★★<br>★ |
| ★<br>★★<br>★ = **3**<br>★<br>★ | ★<br>★<br>★★ = **267**<br>★<br>★★ | ★<br>★<br>★★ = **531**<br>★★<br>★★ | ★★<br>★★<br>★★ = **795**<br>★★<br>★ |
| ★<br>★<br>★★ = **36**<br>★<br>★ | ★<br>★★<br>★ = **300**<br>★★<br>★ | ★<br>★★<br>★ = **564**<br>★★<br>★★ | ★★<br>★<br>★★ = **828**<br>★★<br>★★ |
| ★<br>★<br>★ = **69**<br>★★<br>★ | ★★<br>★<br>★★ = **333**<br>★<br>★ | ★<br>★★<br>★★ = **597**<br>★<br>★★ | ★★<br>★★<br>★ = **861**<br>★★<br>★★ |
| ★<br>★<br>★ = **102**<br>★<br>★★ | ★<br>★★<br>★ = **366**<br>★<br>★★ | ★★<br>★<br>★ = **630**<br>★★<br>★★ | ★★<br>★★<br>★ = **894**<br>★<br>★★ |
| ★★<br>★★<br>★ = **135**<br>★<br>★ | ★★<br>★<br>★ = **399**<br>★★<br>★ | ★★<br>★<br>★★ = **663**<br>★<br>★★ | ★<br>★★<br>★★ = **927**<br>★★<br>★★ |
| ★<br>★★<br>★★ = **168**<br>★<br>★ | ★★<br>★<br>★ = **432**<br>★<br>★★ | ★★<br>★★<br>★ = **696**<br>★<br>★★ | ★★<br>★★<br>★★ = **960**<br>★★<br>★★ |

## 32 Shall my Wife have a **Son** or a **Daughter**?

| | | | |
|---|---|---|---|
| ★ / ★ / ★ / ★ / ★ = 993 | ★ / ★ / ★★ / ★★ / ★ = 233 | ★★ / ★★ / ★★ / ★ / ★ = 497 | ★★ / ★★ / ★ / ★★ / ★ = 761 |
| ★★ / ★ / ★ / ★ = 2 | ★ / ★ / ★ / ★★ / ★★ = 266 | ★ / ★★ / ★★ / ★★ / ★ = 530 | ★★ / ★ / ★★ / ★★ / ★ = 794 |
| ★ / ★★ / ★ / ★ / ★ = 35 | ★ / ★ / ★★ / ★ / ★★ = 299 | ★ / ★ / ★★ / ★★ / ★★ = 563 | ★★ / ★★ / ★★ / ★ = 827 |
| ★ / ★ / ★★ / ★ / ★ = 68 | ★ / ★★ / ★ / ★★ / ★ = 332 | ★ / ★★ / ★ / ★★ / ★★ = 596 | ★★ / ★ / ★★ / ★★ = 860 |
| ★ / ★ / ★ / ★★ / ★ = 101 | ★★ / ★ / ★★ / ★ / ★ = 365 | ★ / ★★ / ★★ / ★ / ★★ = 629 | ★★ / ★★ / ★ / ★★ / ★★ = 893 |
| ★ / ★ / ★ / ★ / ★★ = 134 | ★★ / ★ / ★ / ★★ = 398 | ★ / ★ / ★★ / ★★ = 662 | ★★ / ★★ / ★★ / ★ / ★★ = 926 |
| ★★ / ★★ / ★ / ★ / ★ = 167 | ★★ / ★ / ★★ / ★ = 431 | ★★ / ★ / ★★ / ★ / ★★ = 695 | ★ / ★★ / ★★ / ★★ / ★★ = 959 |
| ★ / ★★ / ★★ / ★ / ★ = 200 | ★★ / ★ / ★ / ★★ = 464 | ★★ / ★★ / ★ / ★ / ★★ = 728 | ★★ / ★★ / ★★ / ★★ / ★★ = 992 |

| | |
|---|---|
| **1** | As the glorious sun eclipseth the light of the stars, so will the partner of thy bed be accounted the fairest among women. |
| **2** | She shall have sons and daughters. |
| **3** | Thy friend is in good health; his thoughts are, at present, bent on thee. |
| **4** | Thou hast no enemies, who can in any degree injure thee. |
| **5** | Choose that for which thy genius is best adapted. |
| **6** | Set not thy mind on searching after that which hath been hidden; but attend diligently to the duties of thy calling. |
| **7** | Choose right trusty companions for thy intended journey, and no ill can befal thee. |
| **8** | Despair not: thy love will meet its due return. |
| **9** | Take not the advice of ignorant pretenders to the art of healing, but apply, at once, to the fountain head of knowledge. |
| **10** | Thy husband will follow arms. |
| **11** | Look for the approbation of the virtuous, and heed not the evil report of the wicked. |
| **12** | O man! be prepared for any change of fortune which may happen. |
| **13** | It signifieth a speedy marriage. |
| **14** | Though fortune now turn her back upon thee; thine own exertions will soon enable thee to triumph over her capricious humour. |
| **15** | Bestow careful culture on the sapling, and when the tree arriveth at maturity, it will produce good fruit. |
| **16** | Let not busy and meddling persons, who call themselves friends, disturb the happiness of the married pair. |

| | |
|---|---|
| **17** | Take heed that thou givest no just cause for thy beloved to prove inconstant to thee. |
| **18** | No impediment will be thrown in the way of the stranger's quick return. |
| **19** | The sceptre of power will be wrested from the conqueror. |
| **20** | The recovery of thy goods will be unexpected. |
| **21** | When thou hast *proved* thy friend, thou mayest truly trust and value him. |
| **22** | How expectest thou to live in the remembrance of thy fellow-mortals, seeing thy deeds are evil? |
| **23** | Let not caprice mar thy happiness. |
| **24** | Be not buoyed up by hopes of inheriting property which thou hast not earned. |
| **25** | Be prudent, and success will attend thee. |
| **26** | Be contented with thy present fortune. |
| **27** | Fortune favours the brave and enterprising. |
| **28** | Thy adversary will cheat thee, on the first opportunity. |
| **29** | Justice is blind, but not always deaf: for in many parts, she loveth to listen to the sweet ringing of gold and silver. |
| **30** | Avoid entering into the land of strangers. |
| **31** | As thy youth may have been virtuous, so will thine old age prove respected and happy. |
| **32** | The captive will speedily cease to breathe the foul air of a dungeon; let him use his freedom wisely. |

| | |
|---|---|
| **33** | The door of the dungeon, will speedily be unlocked. |
| **34** | Consult thy present condition, whether it be right in thee to marry! |
| **35** | She shall have a son, who will gain much wealth and honour. |
| **36** | Thy friends are well; and are now occupied in promoting thy welfare. |
| **37** | Thou hast, and thou oughtest to be on thy guard. |
| **38** | Choose that of thy richest relative. |
| **39** | Disappointment and vexation will attend thee, if thou neglect thy calling, to look after that which is not within thy power to find. |
| **40** | Implore the aid of Providence, ere thou settest thy foot without the threshold of thy house. |
| **41** | The heart of thy beloved yearneth toward thee. |
| **42** | Let proper medicines be prescribed for the patient, and certain recovery will be the consequence. |
| **43** | Thy husband will have many virtues, but also some faults; teach him to correct the latter, and fortune will attend you both. |
| **44** | Thy character will be proof against every ill report. |
| **45** | Let thy heart be cheered under thy misfortunes, for prosperity will return to thee in due season. |
| **46** | The signification is *increase of riches*. |
| **47** | Recovery from thy misfortunes will be gradual, but neglect no opportunity of honestly advancing thine own interests. |
| **48** | If thou wishest thy children to be happy, let thy precepts and practice be both in favour of virtue. |

| 49 | If misfortunes occur, bear them with fortitude, and happiness will be the certain issue. |
| 50 | Be thou constant, and fear not. |
| 51 | Matters which concern the absentee's future happiness, prevent his immediate return. |
| 52 | A conqueror of noble mind and mighty power, shall spring from low condition; he will break the chains of the oppressed, and will give liberty to the nations. |
| 53 | The thief will be detected in the midst of his career. |
| 54 | If thy friend hath in one circumstance proved deceitful, trust him not a second time. |
| 55 | The deeds of the evil-doer will be held in execration by posterity. |
| 56 | Take heed that avarice prove not the bane of thy happiness. |
| 57 | The *will* of a stranger may be written in thy favour. |
| 58 | Be not discouraged by adverse circumstances. |
| 59 | Be just in thy dealings, and trust to Providence for advancement. |
| 60 | Nothing venture, nothing win! |
| 61 | Bet nothing on the result of a game played by others. |
| 62 | God will support thee in a good cause. |
| 63 | Thy wealth will not be gained in a strange land. |
| 64 | The end of dissipation is speedy death—avoid this and live long. |

| | |
|---|---|
| **65** | Early to bed, early to rise, make a man healthy, wealthy and wise. |
| **66** | The prisoner will speedily be released. |
| **67** | Good-temper and fidelity are all thou mayest depend on. |
| **68** | She shall have a daughter, who will inherit all her mother's virtues. |
| **69** | Sickness is not entirely absent from the mansion of those whom thou enquirest after; they say that thy presence would be agreeable. |
| **70** | Thou hast an enemy who will attempt to injure thee. |
| **71** | Tread in thy parent's footsteps. |
| **72** | Spend not thy substance in seeking after that which is not. |
| **73** | Ere thou stirrest abroad, put thine affairs in order, and when thou returnest from thy journey, thou shalt find thy goods secure. |
| **74** | The love which ye bear each other, will be rewarded by a happy marriage. |
| **75** | As thou hopest for a speedy recovery, follow not the advice of the tampering charlatan. |
| **76** | The man of thy heart will not be rich; but his person will be well favoured, and he will give thee every satisfaction. |
| **77** | No man ever was, or ever will be without enemies:—but, those who slander thee, shall be taken in their own nets. |
| **78** | If thou goest to a far country, thy lot will be to undergo many perils. |
| **79** | It portendeth death among thine enemies. |
| **80** | There be many who sink under the burthens of this life; be not thou one of them, but exert thyself and prosper. |

| | |
|---|---|
| **81** | As thou desirest prosperity and happiness for thy children, teach them to avoid evil company. |
| **82** | By this marriage, if thou art prudent, thou wilt gain much happiness. |
| **83** | Give not credit to the insinuation that thy beloved will prove untrue. |
| **84** | The traveller will soon return in good health. |
| **85** | The Islanders who have long swayed the sceptre of the ocean, shall cease to conquer, but they will become the instructors of mankind. |
| **86** | Let not thy hopes of recovering what thou hast lost, be too sanguine. |
| **87** | If thou seest the man whom thou callest thy friend, carry himself deceitfully or dishonestly towards others, deceive not thyself by thinking he will be faithful to thee. |
| **88** | Let not the love of fame blind thee to the interests of thy fellow creatures. |
| **89** | Thou shalt be happier than heretofore. |
| **90** | Be contented with what thou hast already. |
| **91** | Fortune will shower her favours on thee, if thou couplest justice with prudence. |
| **92** | Hope still! never despair! |
| **93** | Lose not thy time and money, by expecting from the lottery what thou mayest easily obtain from thy business. |
| **94** | When thy ready money is gone, go too: never borrow. |
| **95** | Thou shalt have no gain in a law-suit; be therefore wise and careful. |
| **96** | In a strange land a happy marriage awaits thee. |

| | |
|---|---|
| **97** | Thou shalt have to travel both by sea and land. |
| **98** | Yes! |
| **99** | He will at last be freed from the power of his enemies. |
| **100** | Thou shalt have a fortune with thy partner. |
| **101** | Thou shalt be blessed with a son; who, if duly instructed, will make thine age honourable. |
| **102** | Thy friend enjoys perfect health, and is at present engaged in writing an epistle to a relative. |
| **103** | A secret enemy will endeavour to undermine thy happiness. |
| **104** | Choose one, which, with little labour, will afford thee a comfortable subsistence. |
| **105** | Thy business will produce to thee a mine of wealth, if thou art but careful, and improvest thy time. |
| **106** | Thy journey will be safe, and its object will be attained. |
| **107** | Thy love is not disregarded. |
| **108** | The patient will recover; but let this illness be a warning, in future, to keep due guard over his health. |
| **109** | Thou shalt wed a man on whom great honours will be conferred. |
| **110** | See that thou *deservest* to be well spoken of. |
| **111** | Great vicissitudes await the traveller. |
| **112** | The signification is disaster among thy foes. |

| 113 | Consider whether thou art not, thyself, the cause of thy misfortunes; if so, be more prudent for the future. |
| 114 | Misery will be the sure portion of thy children, if their morals be corrupted by evil communication. |
| 115 | Delay not this union, as, thereby, thy happiness would be retarded. |
| 116 | Thou shalt reign paramount in the affections of the being whom thou lovest. |
| 117 | Let not impatience urge too speedy a return. |
| 118 | As instruction is diffused throughout the world, men of all condition, of every colour, and in every clime, will become free. |
| 119 | With trouble and expense, thou mayest gain thy lost goods. |
| 120 | Honesty is the only bond of true friendship. |
| 121 | Seek not fame in the cannon's mouth. |
| 122 | Supreme felicity is seldom the portion of mortal man. |
| 123 | Thou art the favourite of fortune. |
| 124 | Weigh well the probable result of thy present intentions. |
| 125 | By upright conduct, thou art sure to rise. |
| 126 | Save pence; pounds will save themselves. |
| 127 | Never lend at the gaming table. |
| 128 | Rather sacrifice a shilling, than throw away a pound in litigation. |

| 129 | Do wisely, act justly, and trouble not the judges of the land. |
| 130 | It would be imprudent in thee to embark for a foreign land. |
| 131 | Some men are old even at thirty: take care of thy health, and thou wilt see three-score and ten. |
| 132 | The captive's heart will be made glad. |
| 133 | If thou art careful, thou wilt marry exceedingly well. |
| 134 | Thy wife shall have two daughters, whose virtues and beauty will be the theme of general praise. |
| 135 | Thy friends are now carousing, and wishing thee health and happiness. |
| 136 | Beware of false friends! |
| 137 | Thou mayest write up, shave for a penny; cut hair for twopence. |
| 138 | Vain man! flatter not thyself with the hopes of finding silver and gold in hidden places. |
| 139 | Let the companion of thy journey, be honest as well as brave. |
| 140 | Heed not, if disappointment should mar thy present hopes. |
| 141 | The patient's health will be restored. |
| 142 | Thou shalt wed a man in an exalted station. |
| 143 | Do justly and defy calumny. |
| 144 | If thou settest forth from the land of thy fathers, expect great changes. |

| | |
|---|---|
| **145** | Thy dream sayeth be diligent in thy business. |
| **146** | Mankind are often the arbiters of their own fortunes; be honest, and fail not to take advantage of every circumstance which may improve thine. |
| **147** | Destroy the seeds of vice, and implant those of virtue, in the minds of thy children, and happiness will be the certain issue. |
| **148** | Bethink thee whether thou oughtest now to marry. |
| **149** | Constancy on thy part will meet a due return. |
| **150** | When the object is accomplished, the traveller will assuredly return. |
| **151** | A colony of outcasts will break their chains, and obtain great dominion. |
| **152** | Let not the loss of this thing press heavily on thy mind. |
| **153** | Rely not on those self-styled friends who, like summer flies, buzz about thee in thy prosperity. |
| **154** | A cottage, and content, give more enjoyment than the princely palace of the overturner of kingdoms. |
| **155** | Be contented with thy lot, and there is little doubt of thy happiness. |
| **156** | Be content:–let to-morrow provide for itself. |
| **157** | As thou hopest for success, act not unjustly towards others. |
| **158** | Cast not away thy present prospects in pursuing a phantom. |
| **159** | In thy family be liberal, but in thy business save even a far-thing: four farthings make a penny. |
| **160** | Preserve the greatest equanimity at the gaming table. |

| | |
|---|---|
| **161** | Money may be staked, but goods and lands ought never to be risked at the gaming table. |
| **162** | Thou shalt be involved in a suit; but speedily extricate thyself. |
| **163** | Thou wilt be truly prosperous in thy journey; but stay not abroad longer than is necessary. |
| **164** | Rise early, work, or walk, before you eat, and doubt it not. |
| **165** | The prisoner will soon have cause to rejoice. |
| **166** | Thy partner will be rich: but she will also be proud. |
| **167** | She shall bear a son, whose talents will be of the first order; see that they be well directed. |
| **168** | The health of those thou lovest, is good; they enjoy the sweets of rural happiness, and wish that thou wert with them. |
| **169** | Thou hast enemies, but they will have no power over thee. |
| **170** | Meddle not with the laws of the land. |
| **171** | If thou payest attention to all the departments of thy calling, a fortune awaits thee, greater than any treasure within the country in which thou residest. |
| **172** | Tempt not those whom thou meetest, or hast to deal with, by shewing unto them thy money-bags. |
| **173** | If thy love is true, it will be duly appreciated. |
| **174** | A speedy recovery will be the consequence of properly applied remedies. |
| **175** | Thy husband will be in all respects a good man; it will be his study to render thee the happiest of thy sex. |
| **176** | Let thy conduct be unimpeachable, and thou mayest defy the slanderous tongue. |

| | |
|---|---|
| **177** | Be prudent, and do not depend entirely on thy present good fortune. |
| **178** | Thou wert desired in thy vision to give some of thy superfluity, in charity, to the poor. |
| **179** | Thy present misfortunes shall have but little influence on thy future good fortune. |
| **180** | When thou art cold in thy grave, thy name will be greatly honoured in thy children. |
| **181** | By wedding this person thou ensurest happiness for a long season. |
| **182** | If thy beloved hath proved inconstant to another, think not that she will prove faithful to thee. |
| **183** | Love prompts the traveller's speedy return to his home. |
| **184** | An infant nation shall, by the wisdom of its councils, become the emporium of commerce and the arts. |
| **185** | Thy goods may soon be recovered. |
| **186** | Give out that thou art poor, and see how many, or what friends, will run to serve thee. |
| **187** | Be not the trumpeter of thine own fame: if thy deeds are truly great, posterity will not overlook them. |
| **188** | Whatever occurs, be not discontented. |
| **189** | Hope for the best, but make up thy mind to bear with the worst that may happen. |
| **190** | Save thyself the trouble and expense of entering into a rash and unprofitable speculation. |
| **191** | Be content, and heed not the goadings of ambition. |
| **192** | Parsimony is hateful; yet, a groat saved each day, amounts to more than six pounds a year. |

| | |
|---|---|
| **193** | Be like the bee, and thou shalt reap the honey of industry. |
| **194** | Thou wilt mar it wondrously. |
| **195** | To avoid this evil depends greatly on thyself. |
| **196** | Thy journey, when thou goest, will be to thy advantage. |
| **197** | Long life depends greatly on temperance. |
| **198** | He, who inhabits the dungeon, will escape. |
| **199** | Thy *first* partner will be poor, handsome, and chaste; thy *second* exactly the reverse. |
| **200** | A daughter will be born unto thee, who will possess much beauty; which may prove a snare to her, if early vanity be not duly checked. |
| **201** | Thy friends are not in ill-health, but all things are not at present agreeable to them. |
| **202** | Envious persons will endeavour to impede thy passage through life. |
| **203** | Avoid edge-tools! |
| **204** | Be diligent in thy calling, and puff not thy mind up with false hopes. |
| **205** | As thou journeyest along, commend thyself to God, and he will watch over thee. |
| **206** | If thou art discreet, thou shalt gain the suit on which thy heart is fixed. |
| **207** | Let the advice of the experienced be taken, and health will speedily be restored. |
| **208** | Thou shalt marry a man whose mind will be elevated above his condition. It will be thy duty, sometimes to restrain him. |

| 209 | It will! but out of their own mouths will thy slanderers be condemned. |
| --- | --- |
| 210 | Despair not; though fortune should desert thee, it will be but for a time. |
| 211 | Thou wert told in thy vision, that thy present undertaking will prosper if thou art cautious and vigilant. |
| 212 | Cheer thy heart, prosperity will soon attend thee. |
| 213 | Choose those callings for thy children, for which their talents are adapted; teach them to be virtuous and prudent, and leave the result to God. |
| 214 | Enter not into a state, of which thou hast not well considered the end. |
| 215 | Thy beloved meriteth all thy confidence. |
| 216 | Nothing can happen to retard the stranger's speedy arrival. |
| 217 | The rank weeds which have long infested the gardens of the south, will be plucked out, and the tree of liberty will flourish luxuriantly in their stead. |
| 218 | Leave no means untried to detect the thief. |
| 219 | The man who boasts most his readiness to befriend thee, will, in adversity, be the first to desert thee. |
| 220 | Dip not thy laurels in the blood of the vanquished. |
| 221 | Let not the irritation of thy temper mar thy happiness. |
| 222 | Be courteous to thy kinsman, and he will remember thee. |
| 223 | Take the advice of thy best friend before thou proceedest. |
| 224 | Thou shalt long be prosperous, and thou oughtest therewith to be content: in the end thy unbounded ambition will be thy ruin. |

| | |
|---|---|
| **225** | Thou shalt be fortunate, and meet with preferment in thy business. |
| **226** | Yes! |
| **227** | Dost thou expect to plunge thy hand into the fire and not be burnt? |
| **228** | Do as thou wouldest be done by, and thou wilt save much time and money. |
| **229** | Venture not far from home! |
| **230** | Go to bed with the lamb, rise with the lark, and doubt it not. |
| **231** | A friend will procure his speedy release. |
| **232** | Thy partner's temper will be exemplary: take care that, in all cases, thou imitatest it. |
| **233** | Thy wife shall have a son, who will be both learned and virtuous. |
| **234** | Amusement, at present, occupies the attention of thy friends. |
| **235** | Thou hast an enemy, but thy person and fortune are safe from every attempt at doing thee harm. |
| **236** | If thou art wise, thou wilt not spurn rural felicity. |
| **237** | A treasure awaits thee of which thou hast little expectation. |
| **238** | Danger may threaten thee, if thou sojournest long in a strange land. |
| **239** | The hand of thy beloved will ultimately reward thy affection. |
| **240** | Though the patient escape this time, let him not presume on the strength of his constitution. |

| | |
|---|---|
| **241** | By thy marriage, thou wilt be envied by others of thy sex. |
| **242** | Be prudent, and courteous to all men, and the arrows of slander will be blunted before they reach thee. |
| **243** | It will be thy fate to see many changes. |
| **244** | Thou dreamedst of a wedding which will soon take place. |
| **245** | See that thy misfortunes urge thee not on to drunkenness; —if so, thou wilt never recover from them. |
| **246** | In the training of thy offspring, let thy discipline be strict, but not severe; lose no opportunity of improving their understandings, and in the plenitude of their happiness they will bless thee. |
| **247** | It behoves the party to make a light matter of any impediments which may be thrown in the way of his happiness. |
| **248** | There is no just cause why thou shouldest question the fidelity of the beloved of thy heart. |
| **249** | Though the stranger's stay abroad be long, it will be greatly to his advantage. |
| **250** | When imbecility and folly are laid low, a powerful people will regain the liberty they have lost. |
| **251** | Take not away the life of the man who hath injured thee. |
| **252** | Avoid laying too great a tax on the patience of thy friends: —this is the way to preserve them. |
| **253** | Be not eager to rear the monument of thine own fame. |
| **254** | Matrimony will afford thee much happiness. |
| **255** | Be civil to every man; thou knowest not who may prove thy friend. |
| **256** | Be not purse proud, nor vain-glorious, in the midst of thy good fortune. |

| 257 | Let the star of prudence guide thee in thy course. |
| 258 | There is a tide in the affairs of men, which, taken at the full, leads on to fortune. |
| 259 | Thou shalt not:—but be content and happy. |
| 260 | Taste not! touch not! handle not! |
| 261 | If thou dislikest the law, meddle not with it. |
| 262 | When thou hast occasion, thou mayest proceed confidently. |
| 263 | Old age is attained only by the man who has the resolution to live temperately. |
| 264 | The prisoner will soon be welcomed home, although he now smarts under the power of his enemies. |
| 265 | Thou shalt have a handsome partner. |
| 266 | She shall have a son, whose dutiful conduct in his youth, will ensure thee comfort in thine age. |
| 267 | Thy friends are now occupied in devotional duties. |
| 268 | Enemies will endeavour to subvert thy reputation. |
| 269 | Sell strong liquors; but be careful of often trying their strength upon thyself. |
| 270 | A rich treasure awaits thee. |
| 271 | No accident will befal thee. |
| 272 | Thou art more beloved than thou canst be now aware of. |

| | |
|---|---|
| **273** | The afflicted will soon be freed from pain. |
| **274** | Thy husband will inherit great riches. |
| **275** | Thou wilt be calumniated, but when thy slanderers are confronted, they will be put to shame. |
| **276** | Political changes, will change thy fortune. |
| **277** | Thy vision portendeth, that gifts will be made unto thee. |
| **278** | Strong drink may cheer thy heart now, and make thee forget thy sorrows for a short season; but in the end they will unfit thee for the enjoyment of prosperity. |
| **279** | Lose no opportunity of pointing out to thy children the deeds of virtuous men; and in their emulation of them they will do honour to thy precepts. |
| **280** | Much prosperity will attend the wedded pair. |
| **281** | Harbour not unjust suspicions. |
| **282** | When the stranger hath settled his affairs, he will lose no time in returning to his own country. |
| **283** | The deluder of his people will be caught in the meshes of the cunningly contrived net, which he himself hath woven. |
| **284** | Give not the thief the chance of again robbing thee. |
| **285** | Consider well, ere thou tellest thy secret, whether thy friend can keep it. |
| **286** | Do good, and if mankind should fail to remember thee, thou art still their benefactor. |
| **287** | Think not of enjoying happiness whilst thy conduct needs reformation. |
| **288** | Be a friend to thyself:—depend not on others. |

| | |
|---|---|
| **289** | Wish not for the death of thy kinsman, that thou mayest inherit his wordly goods. |
| **290** | Avarice is the ruin of thousands. |
| **291** | Perseverance conquers every impediment. |
| **292** | Thou art too ambitious. |
| **293** | Thou mayest be successful:—millions have been ruined. |
| **294** | Thy fate is to litigate, but in the end thou wilt be successful. |
| **295** | If thou tarriest long from thy home, thy fortune will not prosper. |
| **296** | Drunkenness brings on premature old age: avoid it, and you will live long. |
| **297** | With much difficulty he will obtain a discharge from his prison. |
| **298** | Your partner will, in time, have much money:—use it well. |
| **299** | A daughter will be born unto thee, who will be highly honoured and respected. |
| **300** | Thy friend is well;—he now drinketh thy health. |
| **301** | Thou hast enemies, but thou shalt defeat them, and they will be overwhelmed with shame. |
| **302** | Thou may'st make a fortune by dealing in precious stones. |
| **303** | Health will be to thee the richest treasure thou canst ever possess. |
| **304** | Safety, and success in thy travels, will greatly depend upon thy conduct towards those whom thou meetest. |

| 305 | Persevere, and give not thy suit up lightly. |
| 306 | Let all proper means be used, and speedy end will be put to the patient's disorder. |
| 307 | By marriage, thy fortune and happiness will be greatly increased. |
| 308 | When the evil report reacheth thine ears, instantly find the slanderer out, and he will be confounded in thy presence. |
| 309 | Whatever changes thou mayest undergo, they will be for thy benefit. |
| 310 | It sayeth that favours will be conferred on thee forthwith. |
| 311 | As thou hopest for lasting prosperity, drown not thy cares in strong drink; if thou dost, thy prospects will be for ever blasted. |
| 312 | Their happiness will depend solely on the instruction which thou givest them. |
| 313 | Be discreet in the connection which thou formest for life. |
| 314 | The suspicious lover is the destroyer of his own peace. |
| 315 | When the absentee returns, it will be with joy and honour. |
| 316 | Ignorance and oppression, like a thick mist on the mountain top, will be gradually dispersed, as the sun of knowledge enlightens the understandings of men. |
| 317 | Admonish, but pursue not unto death, him who hath injured thee. |
| 318 | Never trust those men who swear friendship to thee over the cup of drunkenness. |
| 319 | The good deeds of men are frequently traced on sand; their bad ones graven marble. |
| 320 | Set not thy heart on pleasures derived from terrestrial objects. |

| | |
|---|---|
| **321** | Peace and plenty will be thy certain portion, if thou art industrious. |
| **322** | Whilst thou waitest for dead men's *old* shoes, thine own exertions might procure thee *new* ones. |
| **323** | Let prudence guide thee in this affair. |
| **324** | Preferment depends entirely on thyself. |
| **325** | Doubt it not! |
| **326** | The chances are three to one against thee. |
| **327** | Avoid law as thou wouldst the pestilence. |
| **328** | In another country fortune will shower her favours on thee. |
| **329** | Length of days depends greatly on thy habits:—if thou dost not gormandize, nor tipple, thou wilt live long in the land. |
| **330** | The prisoner will find much difficulty in obtaining pardon. |
| **331** | Thou wilt marry into a rich and respectable family. |
| **332** | A beautiful male child will be born unto thee. |
| **333** | Thy friend is happier and in better health than usual; and is preparing for a journey. |
| **334** | Thou wilt be invested by secret enemies, but they will be caught in the trap which they prepared for thee. |
| **335** | Be a miller, but grind not the faces of the poor. |
| **336** | Thou shalt possess a rich mine, out of which treasure shall be dug from time to time. |

| 337 | Prosperity will surely attend thee. |
| 338 | Consider whether the object of thy affections doth deserve thy love. |
| 339 | Fear not but that the patient will recover. |
| 340 | Thy husband will be a man of honour and integrity. |
| 341 | Thy reputation will not be seriously injured by calumny. |
| 342 | Look not on the present as the most important period of thy life. |
| 343 | It signifieth prosperity to thee and thine. |
| 344 | When thy misfortune press hardest on thee, be not dismayed, but endeavour to remove them. |
| 345 | If thy child be permitted to stray from the paths of virtue, thou mayest expect that vice and misery will be his portion through life. |
| 346 | Marriages patched up hastily end in sorrow:—not so those which are prudently contracted. |
| 347 | The object of thy affections will never requite thy love with ingratitude. |
| 348 | Fear not but that the stranger will speedily return. |
| 349 | Shouts of 'Freedom!' will resound throughout the halls which once were filled with the sighs and groans of despair. |
| 350 | Leave no means untried to make good thy loss. |
| 351 | Beware lest the honeyed words of the hypocrite and the deceiver betray thee into danger. |
| 352 | Take good heed!—infamy is the certain portion of the wicked man. |

| | |
|---|---|
| **353** | Thy name will be handed down, with the memory of thy deeds to the most distant posterity. |
| **354** | There is every prospect of happiness for thee. |
| **355** | Depend not entirely on the present intentions of thy kinsman:—they may alter. |
| **356** | Success will depend much on perseverance. |
| **357** | Thou shalt meet with many obstacles, but at length thou shalt attain the highest earthly power and honour. |
| **358** | Industry, perseverance, and circumspection, will accomplish thy most sanguine wishes. |
| **359** | Play no games of hazard. |
| **360** | Law is a two-edged sword, which will assuredly smite thee, if thou comest within its reach. |
| **361** | Remain at home, and thou wilt do well. |
| **362** | A frugal repast will preserve thy health, and give thee many days to live; whilst the midnight banquet may kill thee straight. |
| **363** | Once more will the captive breathe the air of freedom. |
| **364** | Thy partner will be strictly virtuous:—see to it that thou be so likewise. |
| **365** | Thou shalt have a son, whose health in his childhood will require much care. |
| **366** | Thy friends are making merry, and wish thee to form one of their circle. |
| **367** | Thou hast; but they will be discomfited. |
| **368** | Thou art cut out for a rope-dancer. |

| | |
|---|---|
| **369** | Contentment is a richer treasure than any other thou canst find. |
| **370** | Associate not thyself with wicked companions, and thy journey will be accomplished in safety. |
| **371** | Wait patiently, and thy love will be requited in due season. |
| **372** | Let not old women, who pretend to medical knowledge, tamper with the patient's constitution. |
| **373** | Thy husband's conduct will be such as to merit from thee every kindness. |
| **374** | If thou actest prudently and uprightly, thou needest not fear the tongue of the slanderer. |
| **375** | As the seasons vary, so will thy fortune. |
| **376** | It sayeth, 'Let not the next opportunity escape of advancing thy fortune.' |
| **377** | Let not depair be added to the burden of thy misfortunes, but hope that they will be removed in due time. |
| **378** | If thou gainest the confidence of thy children, thou mayest lay the foundation of their happiness, by teaching them to discriminate between good and evil. |
| **379** | If avarice, or mere lust prompt the marriage, expect not lasting happiness. |
| **380** | As the sun steadily pursueth his glorious course in the heavens, so will thy beloved remain constant to her vows. |
| **381** | Thou shalt soon behold the face of the stranger. |
| **382** | A vast empire in the west will burst the chains which fetter it. |
| **383** | If thou art careful, the property may soon be found. |
| **384** | The gripe of the hand, the kiss on the cheek, and the vow of friendship, over the flowing bowl, are but as words traced on the sand of the sea-shore:—trust them not. |

| | |
|---|---|
| **385** | Place not thy confidence so much even in a friend, as to put a weapon in his hand which he may, in future, turn upon thyself. |
| **386** | Thy fame will resound to the farthest corners of the earth. |
| **387** | Prosperity awaits thee. |
| **388** | Thine own industry will supply every want; but if property be bequeathed thee, be thankful. |
| **389** | If thou managest discreetly, thou shalt be successful. |
| **390** | Thou shalt be preferred. |
| **391** | In ten years from this time, (unless by too little dependance on thyself, thou drive fortune from thy door), thou shalt be called a rich man. |
| **392** | If thou art wise, give to the poor, what thou art content to throw away on the turn of a card. |
| **393** | Law leaves little for the litigant:—thou wilt gain thy cause, but the cost will be greater than it is worth. |
| **394** | Tarry with thy friends, and thou wilt escape many calamities. |
| **395** | The shipwrecked mariner may escape the raging billows, and the thief the gallows-tree; but sudden death is the sure portion of the glutton and the drunkard. |
| **396** | If much exertion be used he will obtain his liberty. |
| **397** | A rich and young person will be thy partner. |
| **398** | She shall bear a son, who will reflect much honour on his family. |
| **399** | Thy friend is free from all bodily illness, and now listeneth to the sweet sounds of music. |
| **400** | The enemies who conspire against thee, will be brought to shame and punishment. |

| 401 | Thou mayest be a merchant; but sell not thy soul for gain. |
| 402 | It will be thy fate to pass by, but not to find, a treasure. |
| 403 | Put not thy trust in the fair appearance of all those whom thou meetest in thy travels. |
| 404 | Thou art sincerely beloved. |
| 405 | Let not expense be an obstacle to the restoration of the patient's health. |
| 406 | Consider well whether thou oughtest, at present, to change thy condition in life. |
| 407 | Be more careful to deserve a good reputation by acting virtuously, than merely to avoid the petty calumnies of the envious slanderer. |
| 408 | It is decreed that thy life will be chequered by many vicissitudes; but ultimately, thou shalt enjoy peace and comfort. |
| 409 | It signifieth a gift from a far country. |
| 410 | Thy misfortunes are but temporary. |
| 411 | Point out to thy children the deformity of vice, and they will shun it. |
| 412 | When thou art wed, insist not too much on prerogative, but let each yield a little. |
| 413 | Let not distrust mar thy happiness. |
| 414 | When the time of his sojourning in a foreign land is past, he will return. |
| 415 | As the volcano bursts with a louder explosion, when the combustible matter is confined within its bosom, so will a nation's revenge find vent, the more their wrongs are repressed. |
| 416 | The person who hath wronged thee will be cut off in the midst of his wickedness. |

| 417 | The thief may be successful for a time, but in the end is certain death. |
|---|---|
| 418 | Be exceedingly cautious in the choice of thy friend. |
| 419 | Let thy deeds deserve praise, and posterity will applaud them. |
| 420 | Thy harvest of plenty and happiness is ready; thou must reap it with the sickle of industry. |
| 421 | Bless the memory of the giver! |
| 422 | Be on thy guard against unforeseen events. |
| 423 | Be contented with thy present lot. |
| 424 | Enter into no rash speculations. |
| 425 | Be warned! from henceforth, never play for money, nor money's worth. |
| 426 | When thou understandeth thoroughly the grounds of thy suit, proceed justly, and in the end thou wilt triumph. |
| 427 | If thou art prudent, fortune awaits thee open-handed, in another country. |
| 428 | O man! if thou wouldest see length of days, eschew drunkenness, gluttony, and all intemperance. |
| 429 | The prisoner's release is uncertain:—let some kinsman interest himself in his behalf. |
| 430 | Thou wilt marry one, who hath before tasted the sweets of matrimony. |
| 431 | She will have a son who will live to a great age. |
| 432 | Thy friends are in good health; they have just heard news from a far country. |

| 433 | Enemies thou hast; but their designs will be frustrated. |
| 434 | Love not gold so much as to be an usurer. |
| 435 | If thou takest care to acquire knowledge, it will prove a rich treasure, of which no one can deprive thee. |
| 436 | When thou hast arrived at thy place of destination, lose no time in executing thy errand and return without delay. |
| 437 | Thou shalt receive proofs that thou art beloved. |
| 438 | Put faith in no advice save that of experience. |
| 439 | Thy husband's talents will promote him to honour and to great trust. |
| 440 | At one period of thy existence, attemps will be made to misrepresent thy conduct in the eyes of the world. |
| 441 | A peaceful life is ordained for thee. |
| 442 | It importeth health and happiness. |
| 443 | Be not discouraged though thou art now engulphed in misfortune, thy spirits will soon be buoyed up by prosperity. |
| 444 | Discourage deceit in thy child; but at the same time teach him prudence, that he may not be deceived by others. |
| 445 | To bear and forbear, is the grand secret of matrimonial happiness. |
| 446 | Take heed that jealousy prove not the bane of thy happiness. |
| 447 | The traveller will return richly laden. |
| 448 | Whilst the winds are still, and the air serene, the earth may quake suddenly, and those on its surface be swallowed up. |

| | |
|---|---|
| **449** | After much rain, there will be a plentiful harvest. |
| **450** | Exert thyself manfully to recover the property which thou hast lost. |
| **451** | Try thy friend before thou trustest him too deeply. |
| **452** | If thy deeds are evil, posterity will execrate thy name. |
| **453** | Let not thy exertions flag, and thou wilt be prosperous. |
| **454** | See that thou are not cheated out of thy just rights. |
| **455** | Fear not, if thou art prudent. |
| **456** | Thou shalt be exalted above thy fellows. |
| **457** | Mind what thou art about, and thou art sure to be successful. |
| **458** | If it will afford thee pleasure to behold thyself and family reduced from comfort to beggary,—play! |
| **459** | Send thy cause before a jury of thy countrymen. |
| **460** | If thou remainest in thine own country, thou mayest still be successful. |
| **461** | I have seen the rich man bestow all his goods in charity, and have known the sun to be wholly darkened, but have never yet beheld the hoary locks and healthy aspect of an intemperate man. |
| **462** | Enlargement for the unfortunate captive! |
| **463** | A rich partner, but of a very bad temper. |
| **464** | A son will be born unto thee, who will possess great riches. |

| | |
|---|---|
| **465** | Thy friends are well, but have anxiety concerning thee. |
| **466** | Be thou vigilant, and the designs of those who would do thee mischief, will be defeated. |
| **467** | Knowest thou that, which in the shortest time will be productive of most profit to thee? |
| **468** | It is decreed that thou shalt find another's property; but it behoves thee to restore it to the right owner. |
| **469** | Those who are with thee, will guard over thy safety. |
| **470** | Give further proofs of attachment to thy beloved, and a due return will be made thee. |
| **471** | The patient may look forward to length of days. |
| **472** | Many of thy sex will envy thee the possession of so comely and so kind a husband. |
| **473** | The slanderous reports of thine enemies will not affect the stability of thy reputation. |
| **474** | When thou least expectest, a beneficial change will take place in thy fortune. |
| **475** | It signifieth recovery from illness. |
| **476** | Apply thyself steadily to improve thy fortune, and success will crown thy endeavours. |
| **477** | Train thy child in the way in which he should walk, and when he is old he will not depart from it. |
| **478** | It is folly in thee to wed, if thou hast nothing but mere beauty, or love, to feed upon. |
| **479** | Live cheerily, work merrily, watch warily, but suspect not lightly. |
| **480** | Riches, happiness, and honour, will be in the train of the returning stranger. |

| | |
|---|---|
| **481** | Thy hopes, for the stranger's speedy return, are not well grounded. |
| **482** | The governments of nations will be speedily changed. |
| **483** | Punish not the delinquent too severely. |
| **484** | Thy *friend* will assuredly prove faithful to thee. Is *he* thy friend? |
| **485** | Be honest, and content with the praise of thy contemporaries. |
| **486** | Fail not by persevering industry, to fill thy barns with grain, and thy purse with money, in case of need. |
| **487** | When thou takest possession of the wordly goods of the deceased, do justice to the widow and the orphan. |
| **488** | Venture not rashly. |
| **489** | Thy preferment will be owing to thine own deserts. |
| **490** | When thou hast amassed £10,000,—retire! |
| **491** | Why stake thy fortune,—thy happiness,—thy very existence, on the cast of a die, or the turn of a card? |
| **492** | Be thou thine own advocate. |
| **493** | When thou dost travel, Providence will protect thee. |
| **494** | Thou wilt fondle o'er thy children's children. |
| **495** | After long imprisonment he will be released. |
| **496** | Your partner will be a pattern of virtue and beauty. |

| | |
|---|---|
| **497** | Thou shalt have a son, who shall inherit all his mother's accomplishments, and his father's virtues. |
| **498** | Doubt not but that thy friends are well and happy; they now relish the sweets of a simple but plentiful repast. |
| **499** | The designs of the man who will become thine enemy shall not prevail against thee. |
| **500** | Follow the plough. |
| **501** | Thou shalt assuredly find something, but it will not be of much value to thee. |
| **502** | Linger not unnecessarily on the road, lest danger befal thee. |
| **503** | Thou art beloved; but improve thy opportunity, for delays are dangerous. |
| **504** | A speedy abatement will take place in the patient's disorder. |
| **505** | The mind and the complexion of thy husband will be that of the fox; his practices those of the wolf. |
| **506** | The slander which is uttered against thee will not be credited. |
| **507** | Be not dismayed if misfortune should overtake thee; she will not long keep thee company. |
| **508** | It saith thou hast enemies who are endeavouring to render thee unhappy. |
| **509** | Thy misfortunes are not so great, but that thy own exertions may relieve thee. |
| **510** | Cherish the seeds of virtue in thy children, and doubt not, but in age, they will reap the harvest of happiness. |
| **511** | Exert thyself to make thy partner happy, and thou shalt thyself, be so likewise. |
| **512** | Absence will effect no change in the sentiments of the beloved of thy soul. |

| | |
|---|---|
| **513** | The heart which is penetrated by love for thee, will prove true. |
| **514** | He will soon return, to the great joy of all his friends. |
| **515** | A southern nation will speedily undergo a change in its government, for the better. |
| **516** | A clean corner is not the worse of being twice searched. |
| **517** | Be thine own friend. |
| **518** | Let not a love of fame prompt thee to wicked deeds. |
| **519** | Thy future happiness depends upon thyself. |
| **520** | What hast thou to do with legacies? be industrious and frugal. |
| **521** | Consider well before thou venturest farther in this scheme. |
| **522** | Thine own merits will exalt thee. |
| **523** | Do riches bring content and happiness? |
| **524** | Do not bet high. |
| **525** | Submit to no arbitration, but abide by the verdict of an honest jury. |
| **526** | Thy journey will be prosperous, if guided by prudence. |
| **527** | Thou shalt be termed *venerable*:—see that thy long life be spent usefully. |
| **528** | The bolts will be drawn, the door opened, and the chain will be broken. |

| | |
|---|---|
| **529** | Thy partner will not be handsome, but there will be no other cause for dislike. |
| **530** | A son will be born unto thee, who shall possess much power. |
| **531** | The health of thy friend requireth not the physician's aid; he peruseth a letter just received, which giveth much satisfaction. |
| **532** | An enemy will endeavour to mar thy prospects; but he will be taken in the net which he hath spread for thee. |
| **533** | Seek not the honours nor the dangers of the field. |
| **534** | A good-humoured mate will be a treasure, which thy eyes will delight to look upon. |
| **535** | The companions of thy travels will be unto thee a shield against every danger. |
| **536** | Thou hast the love of others beside that of the darling of thy heart. |
| **537** | Let not the patient by afflicted by melancholy anticipations. |
| **538** | Thy husband will sit in high places. |
| **539** | Evil reports will be uttered against thee, but in due season the slanderer will be discovered, and brought to punishment. |
| **540** | Look well to it, that the lessons which thou receivest in misfortune's school may be useful to thee when thou art prosperous. |
| **541** | It signifieth that thou wilt soon hear agreeable news. |
| **542** | Be patient now, and, in after seasons, prudent.—Thus only canst thou attain prosperity and happiness. |
| **543** | Chastise thy child when he doeth evil, and in the end he will have cause to bless thy name. |
| **544** | Examine strictly the disposition of thy intended partner, and if it accord with thine own, fear not but happiness will attend you both. |

| | |
|---|---|
| **545** | Those who observe truly the vows that have been sworn at the altar, need not fear unhappiness. |
| **546** | Question not the constancy of thy beloved. |
| **547** | He will not return at the time expected. |
| **548** | The present age teems with events of much political import. |
| **549** | Seek, and thou shalt find. |
| **550** | Trust not even a friend with a secret which ought to remain within thine own breast. |
| **551** | Though the present generation may flatter thee, the succeeding one may not be so courteous. |
| **552** | Place not thy happiness in store of gold and silver; but in all thy dealings preserve thy conscience pure and undefiled. |
| **553** | Hope for the best! |
| **554** | Be not buoyed up with the success which may be thy portion. |
| **555** | As the Nile produceth abundant harvests by its annual overflow, so will the good-will of a friend produce thee preferment, fortune, and honour. |
| **556** | Thy speculations will be generally successful. |
| **557** | A lucky hit may make thy fortune:—if so, play no more. |
| **558** | Endeavour to accommodate all differences by the private arbitration of mutual friends. |
| **559** | Thou shalt tarry where thou now residest. |
| **560** | Thou shalt live long; let not thy years be passed ingloriously. |

| **561** | The fettered will soon be free! |
| **562** | A rich partner is ordained for you. |
| **563** | Thou shalt have a daughter, who will possess a noble mind and amiable manners. |
| **564** | The friend whom thou enquirest after, is in good health, and is now locked in the arms of sleep. |
| **565** | See that thy present friends do not become thy determined foes. |
| **566** | Take physic when there is need; but presume not to give it to others. |
| **567** | Be industrious; and place no reliance on such phantasies. |
| **568** | Boast not on the road of the riches which thou carriest with thee, lest they be coveted by others. |
| **569** | Thou art adored; but lose not thy 'vantage-ground by inattention or procrastination. |
| **570** | Let strict attention be paid to the directions given by the medical attendant. |
| **571** | Thy husband shalt have rule, and direction over affairs of great importance. |
| **572** | Give not the slanderer an opportunity of injuring thy reputation. |
| **573** | When thou hast enough, therewith be content, and seek not to enlarge thy store by venturing further. |
| **574** | It signifieth plenty of every thing which gold can purchase. |
| **575** | Though thou art poor and needy, purchase not prosperity by any sacrifice of honesty or honour:—fortune's wheel is constantly turning. |
| **576** | Neglect no opportunity of cultivating the minds of thy children, and their journey through life will be virtuous and happy. |

| 577 | Commit the several members of thy family to the care of an all-seeing Providence, and he will protect them. |
| --- | --- |
| 578 | Mutual love will secure prosperity and real happiness. |
| 579 | Be as constant to thy beloved as she is to thee, and thou mayest be happy. |
| 580 | The stranger will return unexpectedly. |
| 581 | The prudent man will make provision against every change that may take place. |
| 582 | Make proper enquiries, and they will lead to detection. |
| 583 | Shew thy friend, by good treatment of him, that it is his interest to be faithful to thee. |
| 584 | Desire not to attain immortality by the vices of reckless ambition. |
| 585 | Brood not over thy misfortunes, but exert thyself for the future. |
| 586 | Good fortune is in store for thee. |
| 587 | Keep thine own counsel, and success will attend thee. |
| 588 | Neglect not the opportunities which may be offered to thee, for they will lead to great preferment. |
| 589 | A partner in thy business would ruin thee. |
| 590 | Never throw good money after bad. |
| 591 | With the blessing of God thou shalt gain thy cause. |
| 592 | Wander not far from thy home. |

| | |
|---|---|
| **593** | Providence watches over thee, and will lengthen thy days, if thou avoidest the sin of drunkenness. |
| **594** | After a short time, all anxiety for the prisoner will cease. |
| **595** | Thou wilt be exceedingly fortunate in thy marriage. |
| **596** | A son will be born, who if he receive not timely correction, may prove a source of trouble to thee. |
| **597** | The object of thy solicitude is as well in health as thou couldest wish, and is now engaged in domestic occupations. |
| **598** | Beware of treachery! Nothing further may be now revealed to thee. |
| **599** | Cultivate thy talents, and adopt a profession supported by fees. |
| **600** | Thou mayest; but be not disappointed if it be not of great value. |
| **601** | Set out one day, sooner, or later, than thou hadst previously intended. |
| **602** | Your love is mutual, but endeavours will be made to cause dissension between you. |
| **603** | To ensure recovery, the patient's mind must be kept in cheerful mood, by the conversation of those who are most beloved. |
| **604** | Thou shalt wed a man of high birth, but little fortune. |
| **605** | Let justice and prudence be the guardian of thy reputation. |
| **606** | The early part of thy career will be subject to vicissitudes, but in thy age thou shalt enjoy uninterrupted happiness. |
| **607** | It warneth thee to beware of danger. |
| **608** | Sit not down under thy misfortunes, wringing thy hands, and accusing the justice of Providence; but up, and be doing, and fortune will again smile upon thee. |

| | |
|---|---|
| **609** | As the tall column is exalted above the petty ruins which surround its base, so shalt thou rise superior to thy present misfortunes. |
| **610** | If thou hast been prudent and just, thy family will follow thy example, and be happy. |
| **611** | Confidence in each other will ensure happiness. |
| **612** | The heart of thy beloved will find room for no other object but thyself. |
| **613** | The stranger will return at the time thou expectest him. |
| **614** | If the season be unfavourable, let thy exertions be the greater. |
| **615** | Despair not of recovering thy goods. |
| **616** | Wrangle not with thy friend about trifles, else thou mayest forfeit his assistance in matters of great import. |
| **617** | Do justice rather for justice' sake, than to be praised in future ages. |
| **618** | Anticipate not misfortunes before their time. |
| **619** | The money which will be left thee, will not remunerate thy anxiety. |
| **620** | Seek the assistance of a wiser man than thyself. |
| **621** | Eminence is attained by the proper culture of great talents, and preferment, by interest; thy lot is cast between both. |
| **622** | Take a partner, but be not thyself a sleeping one. |
| **623** | Visit a gaming-house; behold the despair of the gamester, who has just lost his all,—and then play. |
| **624** | Thou shalt be foiled by thy opponent's cunning devices. |

**625** In a foreign land strangers will protect and cherish thee.

**626** Desire not so much length of days, as to improve the time which God giveth thee on earth.

**627** The prisoner ought to sue for pardon and mercy.

**628** By this marriage, you will soon obtain great property.

**629** Thy progeny shall be both male and female; they will be the staff and comfort of thy age.

**630** The friend whom thou enquirest after is in excellent health, and is now engaged in conversation with a relative.

**631** An enemy will try to circumvent thee, but he will be foiled in his attempts.

**632** Follow the bent of thine own inclinations.

**633** Domestic felicity will be of more value to thee than the contents of ten thousand mines of gold, silver, and precious stones.

**634** Be not dismayed if thou shouldest meet with danger; it will not affect thee, if thou art resolute.

**635** The heart of thy beloved beateth responsive to the anxious throbbings of thine.

**636** It is useless to look for relief from medicine, unless it be skilfully applied.

**637** The man whom thou weddest shall have great power:— teach him to use it rightly.

**638** When thou art unjustly accused, thy innocence will thereby be confirmed, and the slanderers will be confounded.

**639** Expect not to pass through life without a mixture of good and evil.

**640** It portendeth a happy union between a man and woman, who have long loved each other.

| 641 | Thy nightly visions portend good fortune to thee. |
| 642 | Thy misfortunes shall soon have an end. |
| 643 | Instruct thy children; shew them a good example; and fear not for their happiness. |
| 644 | The marriage will prove both prosperous and happy. |
| 645 | Another will endeavour to supplant thee in the affections of the being whom thou tenderly lovest. |
| 646 | The stranger cannot return at present. |
| 647 | The earth will be fertilized by abundance of rain. |
| 648 | Art thou certain that it hath been stolen? |
| 649 | Reckon not much on the friendship of any man. |
| 650 | Fulfil the duties of thy station, and care not for the unprofitableness of future fame. |
| 651 | If thou continuest virtuous, thou shalt be happy. |
| 652 | Depend not on the caprice of age. |
| 653 | Look before thou leapest. |
| 654 | When thou enjoyest prosperity and honour, feel for the misfortunes of thy former friends. |
| 655 | Have a strict eye over those who eat thy bread. |
| 656 | The companion of blacklegs, cheats, and thieves, even with a fortune, is never respected. |

| | |
|---|---|
| **657** | Venture freely in thy next cause, and gain will crown thy wishes. |
| **658** | Abide thy fate at home; it will be better for thee. |
| **659** | Longevity is a curse to those who mis-spend life. |
| **660** | The prisoner will still pass many days in confinement. |
| **661** | Your matrimonial connexions will not produce much happiness. |
| **662** | Sons and daughters will be the reward of the love which ye bear each other. |
| **663** | Thy friend is now in the act of paying a visit, and is both well and happy. |
| **664** | Thou hast little cause to dread the rage of any enemy who shall come against thee. |
| **665** | Be one of thy country's defenders. |
| **666** | One of thy kindred shall find articles of great value. |
| **667** | The object of thy journey will be attained without hazard. |
| **668** | The heart of thy beloved wavereth between thee and another; improve the opportunities that will be offered thee. |
| **669** | The patient may still hope for health and long life. |
| **670** | Thy husband's horn will be exalted. |
| **671** | Thy innocence will uphold thee in the day of trial, and the tongue of the slanderer will be forever silenced. |
| **672** | Thy voyage through life will at first be boisterous; but the tempest will cease, and propitious winds will waft thee into the haven of independence. |

| | |
|---|---|
| **673** | Thou shalt be subject to a frequent change of residence. |
| **674** | Thy dream signifieth that thou shouldest bestow some of thy goods in charity. |
| **675** | Be not dispirited by misfortunes; they will vanish as the thick mist is dissipated by the genial rays of the reviving sun. |
| **676** | As thou sowest, so shall thy children reap. |
| **677** | Let no petty bickerings disturb the felicity of the married state. |
| **678** | Thy beloved will not cease to pray for thy speedy return. |
| **679** | He will return in due season. |
| **680** | Expect a plentiful harvest. |
| **681** | The thief shall ultimately be detected. |
| **682** | Sad is his fate who relies solely on the friendship and goodwill of others. |
| **683** | Whilst thou seekest to obtain fame, take heed that infamy may not be thy portion. |
| **684** | As the sun revives the flowers of the field, so will prosperity in thy business make thy heart glad. |
| **685** | Blessed is he who expecteth little, for he will not be disappointed. |
| **686** | Examine thyself strictly, whether thou oughest not to abandon thy present intentions. |
| **687** | When thou enjoyest the favour of powerful men, let not thy pride be puffed up. |
| **688** | Thou wilt be the architect of thine own fortune; depend on no created being. |

| | |
|---|---|
| **689** | Be not intoxicated with good fortune at first:—this is the bait which is thrown out by the gamester to allure his prey. |
| **690** | If thou art cozened out of thy upper garment, throw not thy under one away, to recover it. |
| **691** | Let not thy inordinate desire of amassing wealth carry thee into foreign climes. |
| **692** | Desire not to attain old age, if thy mind be not well stored with knowledge:—no wretch is so truly wretched as the ignorant old man. |
| **693** | Some one will pity and release the prisoner. |
| **694** | You will have every cause to love your partner. |
| **695** | A numerous offspring will be born unto thee:—if thou trainest them up properly, their virtues will reward thy anxious toil. |
| **696** | Thy friend is free from all bodily affliction, and expecteth to receive a letter or news from thee. |
| **697** | In a contest which may soon take place, thou shalt be victorious over thine avowed enemies. |
| **698** | Thou wouldest cut but a sorry figure in the pulpit. |
| **699** | Snatch not at shadows; for thou mayest thereby lose thy substance. |
| **700** | If thou meetest danger; face it boldly, and be not daunted by appearances. |
| **701** | Fear not that another will supplant thee in the affections of the beloved of thy soul. |
| **702** | The patient's mind must not be afflicted by doleful intelligence. |
| **703** | Peace, plenty, and happiness will attend thy marriage with the beloved of thy heart. |
| **704** | Deal openly, prudently, and honestly, and thou mayest defy the breath of the slanderer. |

| | |
|---|---|
| **705** | But few persons escape the envenomed tongue of slander. |
| **706** | Thou shalt meet with few vicissitudes. |
| **707** | The interpretation is, that thou shalt receive an epistle of importance. |
| **708** | Thine own exertions will enable thee to overcome every misfortune which may happen. |
| **709** | Lead thy children in the paths of righteousness, and when thou art gone, they will not depart from it. |
| **710** | Happiness depends solely on the affection and forbearance of both parties. |
| **711** | There is danger in long absence from the object of thy affection. |
| **712** | Matters of import, prevent his immediate return. |
| **713** | A revolutionary spirit is abroad among the nations of the earth. |
| **714** | Be patient, and every circumstance will be developed. |
| **715** | If a man protesteth never-ceasing friendship to thee, at least doubt his sincerity. |
| **716** | Sully not thy laurels by unjust deeds. |
| **717** | Carry thyself prudently and justly, and thou wilt surely be happy. |
| **718** | Let not disappointment mar thy exertions in thy calling. |
| **719** | Fortune will attend thee. |
| **720** | When thou art in the zenith of thy power, let not unjust deeds procure thy downfall. |

| **721** | Give not large interest for money in thy business. |
| **722** | If thou playest, play fair, and see that others do the same. |
| **723** | There is great hindrance to thy present success in law matters. |
| **724** | Emigration from thy native land will but retard thy fortune. |
| **725** | Vain mortal! what wouldest thou?—Hoary locks are the reward of temperance and virtue. |
| **726** | Try to unlock the dungeon by means of a golden key. |
| **727** | Be wary, and this marriage may prove very fortunate. |
| **728** | She shall have a son, who in his youth will be admired, and in his old age respected. |
| **729** | Thy friends labour under no bodily affliction, but they are not free from cares concerning wordly matters. |
| **730** | Thine enemies are powerless, and unworthy of thy regard. |
| **731** | On this subject take the advice last given thee by thy best friend. |
| **732** | In this, fortune hath not marked thee for her favourite. |
| **733** | In thy journey, fancy not that from each brake a robber or a tyger will spring upon thee, but pursue thy way steadily. |
| **734** | Success will attend thy anxious hopes, if thou art discreet in this matter. |
| **735** | A speedy cure will depend much on the patience with which the afflicted bears the present illness. |
| **736** | Thy husband will be a man well willed, with a house well filled, and a farm well tilled. |

| | |
|---|---|
| **737** | Thy husband will be learned, his temper good, and his complexion fair. |
| **738** | Thy calumniators will, sooner, or later, be overwhelmed, with shame and disgrace. |
| **739** | If thou tarriest at home, thou shalt meet with few changes. |
| **740** | Thy dream portendeth ill luck to thine enemies. |
| **741** | Thy misfortunes will cease to overpower thee. |
| **742** | Have more anxiety to bequeath knowledge than riches to thy children, and they will be happy. |
| **743** | This union will be productive of real happiness. |
| **744** | Be not neglectful, and thy beloved will remain true. |
| **745** | The traveller will speedily revisit his own country and kindred. |
| **746** | Despotism will speedily be overturned in a country long oppressed by illiterate, indolent, and luxurious strangers. |
| **747** | Make diligent enquiries amongst the members of thy house. |
| **748** | Rely more on the actions, than on the promises of thy friends. |
| **749** | The good deeds of the virtuous only, will be held in esteem by posterity. |
| **750** | Thy misfortunes will vanish, and thou shalt be happy. |
| **751** | Follow thy calling diligently, and be not a legacy hunter. |
| **752** | Rejoice at the fortune which is ordained for thee, and therewith be content. |

| | |
|---|---|
| **753** | When thou enjoyest the favour of the mighty men of the earth, take heed that thou art not ruined by a flattering tongue. |
| **754** | Deal honestly, and trust to God for success. |
| **755** | Mind thy business, and forsake the gaming-table. |
| **756** | Give not large fees in this suit. |
| **757** | In a far country shalt thou find treasure. |
| **758** | If thou art temperate in thine appetites, cleanly in thy person, and just in thy dealings, the winter of thy age will run smoothly. |
| **759** | The captive will suffer no bodily affliction. |
| **760** | This marriage will add to your welfare and happiness. |
| **761** | She will have a son of a forward disposition; but it is thy business to correct, and counsel him aright. |
| **762** | Thy friend is in good health, and hath some thoughts of going on a journey. |
| **763** | Thou hast enemies who speak ill of thee, and who would otherwise injure thee. |
| **764** | Deal in books, and be prosperous. |
| **765** | A good name will prove to thee a treasure of great value:—see thou lose it not. |
| **766** | Tarry not unnecessarily on thy journey:—delays may prove dangerous to thy safety. |
| **767** | A return of affection is at present doubtful, but perseverance and attention will ensure thee success. |
| **768** | Let the patient's mind be soothed by the kind and ready attentions of friends, and the happiest result may be anticipated. |

| | |
|---|---|
| **769** | The patient may recover; but in case of the worst, due preparation ought to be made for the tomb. |
| **770** | Thy husband's temper will be good, and he will make thee happy, if thou dost not attempt to rule over him. |
| **771** | Wert thou chaste as ice, and pure as snow, thou canst not escape calumny. |
| **772** | As the frail bark is tossed on the ocean, so wilt thou be on the stormy sea of life; but in the end thou shalt enter the haven of prosperity. |
| **773** | It signifieth that thou must take heed to avoid danger. |
| **774** | Unlooked-for fortune and happiness await thee. |
| **775** | Teach not thy children to be avaricious, and they will be both contented and happy. |
| **776** | Marriage, when prudently undertaken, is the happiest state into which man can enter. |
| **777** | Fear not that the darling of thy heart will prove inconstant. |
| **778** | He will not tarry long. |
| **779** | A nation accustomed to changes, hath still to undergo a great one. |
| **780** | Blame not thy servant unjustly. |
| **781** | Friends are so scarce, then, when found, they are to be valued above all price. |
| **782** | What brooks fame, if thou hast no fortune! |
| **783** | As the drooping plant is refreshed by the dew of heaven, so will thy heart be gladdened by sudden prosperity. |
| **784** | Divide thy inheritance with those who have an equal right with thyself. |

| | |
|---|---|
| **785** | Rely not too much on present good fortune. |
| **786** | Use no servile means to procure preferment, thou shalt be exalted without their aid. |
| **787** | The eye of a master is worth his two hands. |
| **788** | Avoid every thing that savours of *hell*. |
| **789** | Thy expectations from the law are vain; thou shalt not succeed. |
| **790** | Await thy happy destiny, at home. |
| **791** | It is utter vanity in thee to desire long life, if thy daily habits tend to destroy it. |
| **792** | Cherish and support the poor captive, who will soon be unfettered. |
| **793** | Content will render this union a complete paradise. |
| **794** | Thou shalt be blessed with sons and daughters; but forget not that the tree preserveth the fashion which hath been given to it when a sapling. |
| **795** | A slight disorder affecteth the person, concerning whom thou are solicitous, but it will soon pass away. |
| **796** | The barbed arrow which shall be shot at thee by a secret enemy, will recoil on his own head. |
| **797** | If thou likest *cabbage*, use the needle. |
| **798** | Treasures are but rarely found; throw not thy time away in searching after them. |
| **799** | Comport thyself to the customs of those whom thou meetest on thy journey, and thou shalt meet with little annoyance. |
| **800** | Thou shalt, in time, attain to greater happiness in this matter, than thou canst at present venture to hope for. |

| | |
|---|---|
| **801** | There is much harmony in the love, which thou and the darling of thy heart, bear towards each other. |
| **802** | The patient will assuredly recover from the present illness. |
| **803** | Thy husband will be rich; but his constant aim will be to bear sway over thee, and to keep thee under. |
| **804** | The evil reports of thine enemies will not affect thy character. |
| **805** | Few vicissitudes await thee. |
| **806** | The interpretation is,—that if thou observest any blemish in thine own conduct, that thou shouldest lose no time in correcting it. |
| **807** | Shrink not from encountering whatever may occur to thee; —what thou now deemest misfortune, may ultimately turn to thy advantage. |
| **808** | Instil honour and honesty into the minds of thy children, and fear not for their prosperity and happiness. |
| **809** | Let no one interfere in the domestic feuds of married persons:—if left alone, they will soon subside, and the parties will be happy, as before. |
| **810** | Forget not to keep up an epistolary communication with the beloved of thy heart. |
| **811** | Let preparation be made for his speedy return from abroad. |
| **812** | Where insolent oppression reigns, where tears water the soil, and where sighs fan the scanty harvest, the freed husbandman will sit under his fig-tree, revelling in the joys of abundance. |
| **813** | Accuse not the innocent rashly. |
| **814** | If thou art joined with another in a compact to act wickedly, expect not that he will prove faithful to thee. |
| **815** | The applauses of the wicked are unprofitable, but the praises of the just are like honey which droppeth from the comb. |
| **816** | Correct those faults in thyself which thou seest in others, and thou shalt be happy. |

| | |
|---|---|
| **817** | The legacy that shall be bequeathed unto thee, will not much profit thee, if thou spendest it foolishly. |
| **818** | Lose not thy all, by rash speculation. |
| **819** | Be not servile in adversity, nor despotic in thy prosperity. |
| **820** | Yea! if thou dost steadily avoid the haunts of dissipation. |
| **821** | Better even sleep away thy time, than spend it in ruining thyself or others. |
| **822** | Endeavour to settle all differences in a private manner. |
| **823** | Venture thyself on the ocean, without fear. |
| **824** | The wicked old man is a very wretch, who tastes of hell before his time. Wouldest thou be aged and wicked too? Go to! rather let the sapling wither, than the tree be rotten! |
| **825** | Visit the captive, who is in affliction; but his woes will soon be turned into joy. |
| **826** | Thou shalt marry a very worthy personage, who will inherit considerable property. |
| **827** | As the protecting oak is encircled by the tender ivy, so shall a numerous race of sons and daughters claim thy paternal regard. |
| **828** | Thy friend is in good health, at the present time; he is in the act of bestowing charity. |
| **829** | Act with caution, and thou shalt undoubtedly triumph over a powerful enemy. |
| **830** | Obtain an insight into two trades in which the hands are principally employed; reflect on both for a week, and follow that of which thou dreamest. |
| **831** | Be as industrious as thou art now covetous, and great riches will be thy reward. |
| **832** | Be not affected by the petty inconveniences which thou mayest meet with; else, if thou shouldest be beset with real dangers, thou shalt not have courage to face them. |

| | |
|---|---|
| **833** | Go well armed and accoutred, and dispute not with thy companions on the way, and thy journey will be safe and prosperous. |
| **834** | Thy image is ever before the eyes of thy beloved. |
| **835** | The patient's disorder will yield to proper remedies. |
| **836** | Thou shalt be united to a man whose complexion is dark, but whose features are handsome. |
| **837** | The evil report of thine enemies will recoil on their own heads. |
| **838** | Prosperity will succeed misfortune. |
| **839** | It signifieth that thy conduct requires amendment. |
| **840** | Fear not that misfortunes will continue to pursue thee. |
| **841** | Those concerning whom thou art anxious, will be prosperous and happy. |
| **842** | Let each concede to the other in matters of trifling import, and both will be happy. |
| **843** | Give thy beloved no cause to prove inconstant to thee. |
| **844** | He must still remain a stranger for a short season. |
| **845** | The air which has long been filled with the sighs of oppression, will soon resound with shouts of 'Liberty'. |
| **846** | Be secret, and examine each person singly. |
| **847** | If you expect that a companion in wickedness will prove a faithful friend, thou art deceived. |
| **848** | Enter upon no design of which thou hast not well considered whether it will redound to thy honour. |

| | |
|---|---|
| **849** | Avoid the snares of thine enemies. |
| **850** | Although thou inheritest testamentary property, still be industrious and frugal. |
| **851** | If thou hast enough of earthly goods, therewith be content, and run no risks. |
| **852** | Interest will procure thee preferment to gain trust. |
| **853** | Avoid cards, women and wine,—and prosper. |
| **854** | Thy risks are great, thy chance of gaining small, and in the end, mayhap, thou wilt lose thy all. |
| **855** | Thy gain, at best, will be trivial. |
| **856** | Be steady in thy resolution to turn thy back on thy native shores. |
| **857** | So bear thyself towards thy children and thy kinsfolk, that they may watch over and protect thee, when age weareth thee down, and thy powers fail thee. |
| **858** | The captive will be released, but let him beware of again falling into the clutches of power. |
| **859** | Thou shalt have an honourable, young, and handsome, partner. |
| **860** | Sons will be born unto thee:—train them, in their youth, in the way they should go, and when they are old they will not depart from it. |
| **861** | Thy friend is in the enjoyment of good health, but is not entirely divested of cares. |
| **862** | See that thy conduct be such, that men may love, and not hate thee. |
| **863** | Choose a business in which the hands, rather than the head, are employed. |
| **864** | When thou findest a treasure, teach thy tongue to be silent; and see that thou makest good use of thy riches. |

| | |
|---|---|
| **865** | If thou diggest up thy fields with the plough of industry, thou wilt find a treasure which will reward thy labour. |
| **866** | Thy journey will be prosperous. |
| **867** | Thou mayest hope to gain a place in the affections of the darling of thy soul. |
| **868** | The pain with which the patient is afflicted, will soon be terminated. |
| **869** | Thy husband will be exalted to a high station. |
| **870** | Thy calumniators are busy, but they will be baffled in their endeavours to injure thee. |
| **871** | Great vicissitudes await thee, but they will not much affect thy future fortune. |
| **872** | The signification is, that good luck will befal thee. |
| **873** | Misfortunes may be thy lot in the beginning, but in the end will be peace and happiness. |
| **874** | Fail not, duly to instruct thy children in all knowledge which may be meet for them, and they will assuredly profit in the end. |
| **875** | Mutual forbearance is the strongest bond of matrimonial felicity. |
| **876** | The affections of the being whom thou lovest will be placed on none other but thyself. |
| **877** | He will come back with abundance of riches and knowledge. |
| **878** | He who ruleth the kings of the earth, and who terrifieth the nations with the sound of his arms, will be abased, and speedily cut off. |
| **879** | Be sure of thy grounds before thou enterest on a prosecution. |
| **880** | Choose thy friends only, from among the virtuous; and fear no treachery. |

| 881 | The approval of thy Creator is more profitable than the empty applauses of men. |
| 882 | Be select in the choice of thy friends, and the future will be happier than the past. |
| 883 | Though thou inheritest houses and lands, what availeth it, if thou art not prudent. |
| 884 | Impediments will start up which thou dreamest not of. |
| 885 | Be honourable, and honest in thy dealings, and thou shalt be greatly exalted. |
| 886 | Thou wilt find the benefit of neither giving nor taking long credit. |
| 887 | Leave off play as the clock strikes twelve; after that hour there is no luck for thee. |
| 888 | Expectest thou to snatch the burning oil from the devouring flames? no more think of rescuing thy goods out of the fire of the law, if once it feedeth on them. |
| 889 | Thou shalt visit distant regions, where gold aboundeth:— in thy prosperity, forget not the widow and the orphan. |
| 890 | It is not meet for thee to desire old age, if thou dost too freely indulge thy carnal appetites. |
| 891 | Captivity, anxiety, suspense, liberty, and joy, will rapidly succeed each other. |
| 892 | Thou shalt marry thy equal in worth and fortune:—be content and happy. |
| 893 | As the roses bloom upon the parent tree, so will sons and daughters grace thee by their beauty. |
| 894 | The objects of thy anxious inquiry are well; they are equally solicitous regarding thy welfare. |
| 895 | Thou wilt be envied; but it should be thy constant care, that even thine enemies shall have cause to admire thy virtues. |
| 896 | Choose not a business which dependeth on the whim and luxury of the age in which thou livest. |

| | |
|---|---|
| **897** | Richard Whittington, from small beginnings, by industry, became Lord Mayor of London. Go thou and do likewise. |
| **898** | Lose not time from thy business, in looking after hidden treasures. |
| **899** | Prosperity will attend thy travels, but thou must still be prudent. |
| **900** | Rejoice! Thou art truly beloved. |
| **901** | The patient's disorder will soon be greatly alleviated. |
| **902** | Thy husband will possess great riches. |
| **903** | Let thy reputation be founded in virtue, and thou need'st not dread the rancorous shafts of calumny. |
| **904** | Fear not that fortune will desert thee. |
| **905** | It importeth kindness and charity to thy poor friends. |
| **906** | After rain cometh sun-shine. |
| **907** | As thou hopest happiness for thy children, lead them in the paths of virtue and honour. |
| **908** | Misfortunes may becloud the dawn of matrimony, but the evening will be serene and happy. |
| **909** | Doubt not the vows of love which have been made to thee. |
| **910** | A certain circumstance prevents his immediate return. |
| **911** | Those who have long sighed for freedom shall soon attain it. |
| **912** | When thou hast discovered the thief, see that his punishment be proportionate to his crime. |

| | |
|---|---|
| **913** | If thou expectest thy friend to be true, be true to him. |
| **914** | If thy deeds are just, fear not but that future generations will hold thy memory in esteem. |
| **915** | A man's happiness depends entirely on the company which he keeps. |
| **916** | O man! forget not that the goods which thou inheritest are not of thine own earning; therefore remember the poor in the days of thy prosperity. |
| **917** | Before thou buildest, reckon the cost of thy house. |
| **918** | Thy horn will be exalted above thy fellow. |
| **919** | Rise early, mind thy business, be regular in thy accounts, and prosper. |
| **920** | Never drink until the game is ended. |
| **921** | Verily, it will be vanity in thee to expect success in thy suite. |
| **922** | Fortune will favour thee in thine own country. |
| **923** | Longevity and sensual gratifications are incompatible:— think not of enjoying both. |
| **924** | The captive will at length escape, and triumph over his enemies. |
| **925** | You will marry a person with whom you will have much comfort. |
| **926** | Thou shalt have three lovely daughters; instruct and watch over them, as thou wouldest over the apple of thine eye. |
| **927** | Thy friend enjoyeth health and happiness; he is in the act of telling money. |
| **928** | Heed not the feeble and impotent attempts of him who will attempt to do thee hurt. |

| | |
|---|---|
| **929** | Thou hast enemies who, if not restrained by fear of the laws, would plunge a dagger in thy heart. |
| **930** | The soldier's bayonet hath sometimes given place to the fieldmarshal's baton. |
| **931** | The treasure thou wilt find, will be a partner, whose affectionate heart will share thy happiness, and sympathize in all thy sorrows. |
| **932** | No ill-luck will befal thee. |
| **933** | There is no lack of regard on the part of thy beloved. |
| **934** | The patient's illness will yield to proper remedies. |
| **935** | Thou shalt wed a man of much substance. |
| **936** | Thou shalt be well spoken of. |
| **937** | Be prudent, and thy vicissitudes will bring thee nearer to the happiness destined for thee. |
| **938** | It portendeth danger, if thou art not cautious. |
| **939** | The clouds on thy brow will be dispersed by beams of fortune and happiness. |
| **940** | Restrain thy children when they indulge in wicked courses, and when thou art gathered unto thy fathers, they will have cause to bless thy name. |
| **941** | Fear not that misfortune will attend this marriage. |
| **942** | Thine own fidelity, and that of thy beloved, will be rewarded with happiness. |
| **943** | The stranger will return, but not speedily. |
| **944** | Tyranny will soon be engulfed in the abyss of its own iniquity. |

| | |
|---|---|
| **945** | By perseverance only, shalt thou recover thy goods. |
| **946** | When thou askest advice from thy friend, relate not to him thy story by halves, lest in concealing the matter from him, thou suffer in the end. |
| **947** | In future ages shall thy name be cited as a pattern for rising generations, if thou art the benefactor of mankind. |
| **948** | Avoid the haunts of the wicked, and be happy. |
| **949** | Thine own earnings will prove much sweeter than the largest inheritance. |
| **950** | Be exceedingly cautious in thy present speculations. |
| **951** | Be true in thy present trust, and thou shalt have affairs of much importance committed to thy care. |
| **952** | The industrious man is seldom the fortunate one. |
| **953** | Confine thyself to games, wherein thou mayest overcome thy rival by ingenuity and fair play. |
| **954** | Thou wilt soon obtain what thou little expectest. |
| **955** | If thou goest far abroad, thy kinsmen at home will not deal justly by thee:—tarry not by the way. |
| **956** | Old age never commands respect, unless it be allied with virtue:—wouldest thou be old and detested too? |
| **957** | The captive will live to see his enemies punished. |
| **958** | Thy partner will, if used well, go through every danger for thee. |
| **959** | As the parent trunk giveth up a part of its nourishment to the tender shoots which spring from its sides, so will sons and daughters require thy succour and protection. |
| **960** | Fear not for the health of thy friends; they are in expectation that thou wilt send them some small matter whereby they may keep thee in remembrance. |

| 961 | Thy friends are well, and sleep soundly in the mansion of content and happiness. |
| 962 | Thy enemies will not have power to harm thee. |
| 963 | Make a bold effort to sit on the woolsack. |
| 964 | It will not be thy fortune to discover hidden treasures. |
| 965 | Let prudence be thy guide, and thou wilt reach thy journey's end in safety. |
| 966 | The beloved of thy soul adores thee in secret. |
| 967 | Let every means be used for the restoration of health. |
| 968 | The good temper of thy husband will make thee happy. |
| 969 | Waste not thy time by seeking for the good report of every man. |
| 970 | Man that is born of woman, is born to trouble, as the sparks fly upwards. |
| 971 | It signifieth that thou oughest not to trust another with affairs which thou canst manage thyself. |
| 972 | Let not thy misfortunes unman thee; but prepare thyself for happier times. |
| 973 | When the upright man sleepeth under the sod, happiness and prosperity will attend his offspring. |
| 974 | A marriage founded on avarice is seldom a happy one. |
| 975 | Consult thine own heart, whether thou oughest to have exacted a vow of constancy. |
| 976 | The stranger will return soon. |

| | |
|---|---|
| **977** | The wings of the eagle of the north will be clipped, and his talons blunted. |
| **978** | It is necessary for thee to bear thy loss with fortitude. |
| **979** | One act of disinterested friendship should cancel the remembrance of a thousand foibles. |
| **980** | Abuse not the power which the Lord giveth thee, and thy name will be hailed with rapture in future ages. |
| **981** | Thy misfortunes will soon terminate. |
| **982** | Fear not that thine own industry will procure thee a sufficient provision. |
| **983** | Let prudence and justice be thine handmaids, and all thy undertakings will prove successful. |
| **984** | Kick not down the ladder which raises thee. |
| **985** | A penny saved is a penny got;—a word to the wise is enough. |
| **986** | Effect no mortgage to pay a gambling debt. |
| **987** | Thy hope is vain, justice is blind to thy claims, and fortune shuns thee. |
| **988** | The wealth thou gainest abroad, distribute justly and charitably at home. |
| **989** | To arrive at old age, thou must avoid the causes of premature decay. |
| **990** | Liberty will be proclaimed to the captive. |
| **991** | A handsome good-natured partner, a bag of gold, and a carriage. |
| **992** | A son will be born unto thee, who will not disappoint the hopes which thou shalt entertain respecting him. |

| | |
|---|---|
| **993** | Thy wife will bless thee with a large offspring: and will be among them, as the queen of night among the stars of heaven. |
| **994** | Those concerning whom thou art anxious, are well and happy:—they now enjoy the sweets of conversation. |
| **995** | Thou hast:—but fear not that they will have power to injure thee. |
| **996** | Write on thy door-posts,—*Mangling done here!* |
| **997** | The silver and gold which hath been buried in the earth, will, forever, be hidden from thy view. |
| **998** | When thou goest forth from thy dwelling, no harm will overtake thee. |
| **999** | Thy love will meet its due return. |
| **1000** | Whilst there is life there is hope:—let no means be left untried to cure the disorder. |
| **1001** | An honourable man will wed thee. |
| **1002** | Thy reputation will in a small degree, be affected by detraction. |
| **1003** | Many scenes will be presented before thine eyes. |
| **1004** | It importeth, that if thou dost procrastinate, evil will attend thee. |
| **1005** | Thy misfortunes ought to be thy fortune monitors:— take heed, and prosperity will attend thee. |
| **1006** | To be happy, it is necessary only to be virtuous:—teach this to thy children, and they will be benefitted. |
| **1007** | Care not so much for abundance of gold and silver with thy partner, as stores of virtue and prudence, and thy marriage will a happy one. |
| **1008** | Lay it not greatly to heart, if the being thou now dotest on should prove changeable. |

| | |
|---|---|
| **1009** | The stranger's return will be hailed with joy. |
| **1010** | The storm of revolution will rage throughout the earth for a time; but, in the end, peace and plenty will be diffused among the nations. |
| **1011** | When thou hast recovered thy goods, be careful of them for the future. |
| **1012** | Let not interested persons have so much power over thee as to cause distrust or discord between thy friend and thee. |
| **1013** | Let not thy desire of making thy name live for ever, urge thee on to deeds of cruelty and rapine. |
| **1014** | Happiness and misery are merely relative; therefore make not thyself unhappy for trifles. |
| **1015** | Be not intoxicated with good fortune, when it arrives. |
| **1016** | Rely not on specious appearance. |
| **1017** | Good deeds will prefer thee to honour. |
| **1018** | Envy not thy industrious neighbour, but steadily follow his example. |
| **1019** | Beware of foul play. |
| **1020** | Doth the wolf tamely relinquish his prey, or the fox his booty? How then expectest thou to rescue thy goods from the fangs of the man of law? |
| **1021** | Fear not for thy journey,—it will be prosperous. |
| **1022** | Let temperance be thy nurse, and labour thy physician, and thou will need none other, for health will be the companion of thy age. |
| **1023** | Speedy release for the prisoner |
| **1024** | Your partner will possess houses and lands. |

# INDEX